Railway World SPECIAL

MIDLAND & GREAT NORTHERN JOINT RAILWAY

Cover:
An Ivan Lilley painting of a representative M&GN scene at Sutton Bridge around 1930, showing a 'C' class 4-4-0 crossing the Cross Keys Swing Bridge and about to enter the station. Very few of these locomotives were fitted with Deeley smokebox doors while still in yellow livery but most were so fitted by the time they were brown, in place of the plain Johnson design. Today the bridge carries the major A17 route to the Midlands and has recently been refurbished at a cost of £2.8 million: this is ironic in view of the fate of the M&GN due to the weak West Lynn Bridge just a few miles down the road! *Courtesy J. Barker*

Back Cover Upper:
A typical M&GN through train of the BR era. Ivatt 4MT No 43160 enters Potter Heigham station with the down 'Leicester' in August 1958.
T. Owen/Colour-Rail

Back Cover Lower:
During 1989 BR-built 'J72' class No 69023 *Joem* was loaned to the North Norfolk Railway. Although built in 1951 its design dates back to 1898 when it was introduced by the North Eastern Railway. *Joem* was the second BR steam locomotive to see service on the NNR and on 1 August was standing at Sheringham with the 14.45 for Holt. *Hugh Madgin*

Published by

IAN ALLAN LTD

Terminal House Shepperton TW17 8AS
Telephone: Walton-on-Thames (0932) 228950
Fax: 0932 232366 Telex: 929806 IALLAN G
Registered Office: Terminal House Shepperton TW17 8AS
Phototypeset and Printed by Ian Allan Printing at their works at
Coombelands in Runnymede, England

First published 1990

ISBN 0 7110 1900 2

Published by Ian Allan Ltd, Shepperton, Surrey; and printed by Ian Allan Printing Ltd at their works at Coombelands in Runnymede, England

Contents

Acknowledgements

Having been privileged to serve as Editor of the *M&GN Circle Bulletin* for the past 14 years, there are many people to thank. First our President Ronald H. Clark who introduced me — and many others — to the Circle through his pioneering book *A Short History of the M&GN.* Then there are all the Circle members whose reminiscences and contributions to the *Bulletin* have helped provide an original text. Particular thanks are due to David Bayes for his invaluable aid checking my text, writing the locomotive chapter and assistance providing captions for the illustrations. Also Circle Photo Archives Officer Adrian Whittaker, who helped organise the illustrations, Circle Drawings Officer John Hobden for the diagrammatic maps, David Madden and Chris Cole of the North Norfolk Railway and Midland & Great Northern Joint Railway Society for their friendly co-operation, Circle members Nigel Digby, Richard Adderson and Alan Wells (himself an ex-M&GN driver) for checking the text and correcting my inaccuracies, Times Newspapers Ltd for allowing reproduction of 'Character Sketch of a Railway' and last, but not least, my wife Jill for typing the script.

Photographs are mainly from the M&GN Circle Collection and Ian Allan archives to whom grateful acknowledgement is also made. Ron White of Colour-Rail was also most helpful. Particular thanks are owed to Circle members who made photographs available, and the photographers, all whose names appear under the illustrations where known. Prominent are the ever-helpful H. C. and R. M. Casserley, H. N. James, the late Ted Tuddenham, and faithful recorder of East Anglian byways Dr I. C. Allen — Circle members all.

The colour photographs comprise the most ever published of the M&GN in one volume and, regrettably, transparencies of the Joint before the 1959 closure are very scarce. Should any reader have taken any we would be pleased to hear!

Michael J. Clark
Bedford
1 June 1989

1. Character sketch of a railway

CHARACTER SKETCH OF A RAILWAY

IS IT GOODBYE TO THE MIDLAND AND GREAT NORTHERN JOINT?

FROM A CORRESPONDENT

The closing of railway lines in England grows apace. In many a country parish these last few years it has been the same; as the breaker's men rip the lead from the lord's house, the last train runs on the single track his great grandfather feared and fought, and soon rust will gather on the bright metals.

The latest casualty—and a large one—is the former Midland and Great Northern Joint Railway. Tried and found wanting by the railway authorities, most of it (unless the local opposition to the proposed closure triumphs) seems likely to go the way that other "unremunerative" lines have gone before.

"A product of the extravagant and over-optimistic period of railway development in the nineteenth century," said the indictment with the severity of a Silk prosecuting a swindling secretary, "it was not planned as a whole, but emerged as a through route from various amalgamations of local railways . . . it has never paid its way. . . ." Well, perhaps not, but did the companies in a larger way of business? Certainly, for a railway born with a wooden spoon in its mouth and stingily treated by its owning partners, it did not do so badly.

Controversy apart, what was it like, the old Muddle and Get Nowhere, as impious spirits called it? One says "was," as though it were already dead, but the old M. & G.N. as many of us knew it, seems to have been gone a long time and the use of the past tense is occasionally unavoidable.

NOT A MERE BRANCH

Whatever else it was it was much more than a branch line; even the present owners admit that it became a through route. It was also the owner of 109 miles 18 chains of single line, 74 miles 14 chains of double, an engineering works, a small tunnel, two swing bridges, and some very pleasant scenery. But more than these earthly possessions it had a distinct personality which its name reflected.

Midland and Great Northern. No doubt a system that passed through the green shires where hounds run all winter, through the Dukeries and the grey lands where coal is dug and iron smelted, a Notts and Derby line with a pied-à-terre in the West Riding? By no means; though there was territory in Lincolnshire and in Cambridgeshire, even a station in Northamptonshire, much of the line was in Norfolk—which only the B.B.C. includes in the Midlands.

Yet the name was not altogether inapt for there were—and are—through trains to Birmingham and Leicester by way of Bourne, and to the North or London by way of Peterborough. And certainly in the heyday of the system there were through coaches in the summer from places as far afield as Manchester, Derby, and Sheffield.

Travelling on the M. & G.N. you are treated to none of the renowned scenic splendours of the kind offered by the Big Four; no Lakes or Highlands, no Thames or Tweed, no mills darker or more satanic than those that ground corn in Cotman's day; but if unspectacular the country is unspoiled. For some 50 miles it runs over the fertile Fen plain, and here was trade that summer and winter sent trains rolling away over the dikes and drains bearing tulips and broccoli, cabbages and daffodils, strawberries and currants, and the diamonds of the black soil, potatoes.

From South Lynn you pass through "King's Country," heather and pines and houses of ruddy local stone. "Hillington for Sandringham," says a station sign with a broad hint, hoping no doubt that one day a princeling would entrain not at Liverpool Street but at King's Cross; perhaps one did; but the Royal themselves travelled Great Eastern and went to Wolferton when they came to Norfolk.

Away eastward the line crosses good farming land by the broad acres of the Townshends of Raynham to Melton Constable. The "Crewe of North Norfolk" the wags have called it; but it was scarcely that, for though they built locomotives there in happier days, and all around is unmellowed railway brick, Melton was never a railway town like Doncaster or Swindon.

THE BURGH PARVA COWS

From the main platforms at Melton you can still hear the Burgh Parva cows at milking time, the marshalling yards end in meadowland, and hard by is a noble beech hedge that flanks a road leading to Melton estate, the home for many years of the Lords Hastings. On any one of the three branch lines leading from Melton is something to please the eye; the sea at Sheringham and Cromer, the sea ultimately at Yarmouth, but on that line also Stalham, Potter Heigham, and the Broads.

The third line goes south through woodland and arable to Hindolvestone, Guestwick (which Trollope borrowed for the Barset novels) Whitwell and Reepham, and Lenwade, that village beloved of Parson Woodforde who used to take his pleasure with rod and net in the Wensum near by; and so at length to Norwich and City Station, "the cathedral of the M. & G.N. where a great bell tolled before the departure of trains."

Such is the Midland Great Northern "political and physical," but any remembrance of it would be incomplete without a reference to its locomotives, yellowish of complexion, "picked out in blue with an elaborate achievement of arms upon the tenders, resplendent with fishes and keys in saltire and looking as if they were By Appointment to the Holy See." But many were elegant without benefit of paint and livery, for they were the creations of that artist among railway engineers, Samuel Johnson, of the Midland Railway, who like J. G. Robinson of the Great Central never built an ugly engine.

FAMILIES "ON THE LINE"

Elegant yes, and of obsolete design. But, nevertheless, in the summer season when holiday Brummagem came—and still comes—to Yarmouth and Cromer, they tackle trains of 400 and 450 tons weight, which speaks much for the standard of maintenance at Melton and South Lynn and for the driving and firing of engine crews.

Indeed, one of the great strengths of the M. & G.N. was its servants. It used to be said that on arrival at Paddington you left London and entered Great Westernland where west country speech prevailed; but on the M. & G.N. it was East Anglia almost all the way; the guard, the signalmen, the driver and the porter not only spoke the same tongue but were quite likely to be related by blood and marriage. When the railway broke into the countryside in the nineteenth century, families that had worked on the land time out of mind went "on the line," and there, with East Anglian conservatism, they stayed so that there has been ever since a kind of feudal continuity of service.

Whatever the fate of the railway, it is true to say that within its limitations—among them the elderly locomotives and an overdose of single track—it gave good service to East Anglia and in return East Anglians served it well.

Above:

The heraldic device of the railway containing the blazons of the See of Peterborough, Norwich, of Lynn and of Yarmouth. *M&GN Circle*

An extract from *The Times* dated 18 July 1958.

The M&GN was indeed closed on 28 February 1959.

The following pages seek to illustrate further the character of a much loved and lamented railway line. The concluding chapter relates how the line is remembered today in the form of the preserved North Norfolk Railway and the Midland & Great Northern Circle.

© *The Times* 18 July 1958.

2

2. 'A product of the extravagant and over-optimistic period of railway development in the 19th century'

Railway communication in the district served by the M&GN was, indeed, provided originally by a number of small independent companies. A brief outline of why and how this came about will help explain the rise and fall of the railway. In the 1850s those lines which had been built in East Anglia were under the control of the ill-reputed Eastern Counties Railway (ECR) which already had stations at Wisbech, Lynn, Norwich, Yarmouth, Lowestoft and Peterborough, and consequently claimed this left 'not a single opening for any rival line'.

But this was the era of intense rivalry between railway companies. The Great Northern Railway (GNR) was the first into Spalding (in 1848) but was in conflict with the ECR over running rights in Wisbech which the GNR required to gain access to Lynn and the dock traffic. Thus was conceived the first of the M&GN's predecessors, the Norwich & Spalding Railway in 1852. The method employed was to encourage backing and support from local businessmen. The inclusion of Norwich in the title did not indicate early plans to also build a separate line all the way to the city, but to enable access thereto via Wisbech and the Eastern Counties Railway. However, this did not materialise mainly because of the length of time taken building the line, for it was 15 November 1858 before it was opened to Holbeach and the section to Sutton Bridge was opened on 1 July 1862. Naturally the GNR undertook to work the line.

Meanwhile, a separate company was formed to connect to the GER's station at Lynn, namely The Lynn & Sutton Bridge Railway, and this was opened on 1 March 1866. The line was also extended westwards by the Spalding & Bourne Railway Company and opened on 1 August 1866, operated by the GNR.

On the same date the Peterborough, Wisbech & Sutton Railway (PW&S) was opened and this finally released the Norwich & Spalding Railway from its duty to build a line to Wisbech, for all lines

eventually connected at Sutton Bridge. The PW&S was operated by the Midland Railway (MR), giving it access to Wisbech and Sutton Bridge, whereas the Bourne-Sutton Bridge section was operated by the GNR. Thus the Lynn-Sutton Bridge line was separately courted by the GNR and MR for access to Lynn. Common sense prevailed, for in 1867 joint working by the GNR and MR was agreed by formation of first the Midland & Eastern Company, then the Bourne & Lynn Joint. Therefore as the consequence initially of competition the parent companies worked together west of Lynn, enabling them to both achieve their desire of access to the town.

East of Lynn the predecessors of the rival Great Eastern Railway (GER) were the first to build lines to the major towns, including Yarmouth. Then suddenly in the mid-1870s came a rush of new promotions encouraged by Messrs Wilkinson & Jarvis of Westminster, speculative contractors and engineers. The first line to be built was that from Yarmouth to Ormesby (opened 7 August 1877), extended to Hemsby (16 May 1878), to Martham (15 July 1878), Catfield (17 January 1880), Stalham (3 July 1880) and North Walsham (13 June 1881). Called at first The Great Yarmouth & Stalham Light Railway, then in 1878 the Yarmouth & North Norfolk Light Railway (Y&NN), the use of the term 'Light Railway' was a successful ruse to allay objection from the GER, but one of the promoters, the banker-brewer Sir Edmund Lacon admitted in 1881 that the ulterior motive was to compete with the Great Eastern and go to Fakenham and Lynn. Once again Lynn was the ultimate prize.

During the same decade, the Lynn & Fakenham Railway (whose contractors were once more Wilkinson & Jarvis) was building eastward from King's Lynn. Its line was opened from Gaywood Junction (on the Lynn-Hunstanton branch of the GER) to Massingham on 16 August 1879; and to Fakenham on 16 August 1880. By an Act of 12 August 1880, the company was authorised to extend its line to

Norwich, Holt and Blakeney. The section from Fakenham to Guestwick was opened on 19 January 1882; thence to Lenwade on 1 July 1882; and through to Norwich (City) on 2 December 1882. The Blakeney branch was never built, but it is relevant to observe that the original plan was to terminate the line at the fishing port of Blakeney, not Cromer, as the latter's development as a holiday resort was still a few years away.

This was the position when, by an Act of 18 August 1882, the Eastern & Midlands Railway (E&M) was formed as an amalgamation of the small companies that had remained outside the Great Northern and Great Eastern Railways, comprising the Lynn & Fakenham, the Yarmouth & North Norfolk, and the Yarmouth Union. By the same Act the Midland & Eastern and the PW&S were merged into the Eastern & Midlands system as from 1 July 1883. The Yarmouth Union Railway, incorporated on 26 August 1880, opened a connecting link between the Y&NN and the GER on 15 May 1882.

An extension from Melton Constable to North Walsham having been opened on 5 April 1883, the newly formed Eastern & Midlands group finally had an unbroken system from Bourne and Peterborough to Norwich and Yarmouth. Lynn was still in effect the dividing line, for the GNR and MR continued to operate the lines to the west under the existing arrangements, while the E&M operated the lines to the east of Lynn. It then undertook a branch to Holt which was opened between Melton Constable and Holt on 1 October 1884, and finally extended to Cromer on 16 June 1887. An important connecting loop between South Lynn and Bawsey, via Gayton Road, was opened on 1 January 1886 permitting through working between the eastern and western sections of the system without reliance on the Great Eastern's station at King's Lynn. The old section between Gaywood Junction and Bawsey was thereupon abandoned. The junction with the GER was severed but the

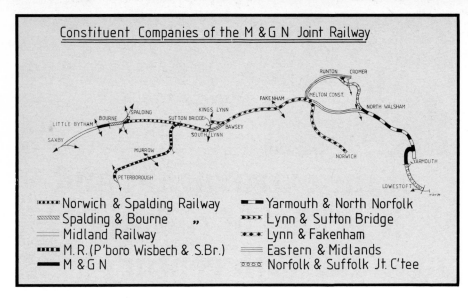

Constituent Companies of the M & G N Joint Railway

Legend:
- ▪▪▪▪ Norwich & Spalding Railway
- ≈≈≈ Spalding & Bourne   „
- ——— Midland Railway
- ▪▪▪▪ M.R.(P'boro Wisbech & S.Br.)
- ▬▬ M & G N
- ▬•▬ Yarmouth & North Norfolk
- ▪▪▪▪ Lynn & Sutton Bridge
- ✱✱✱ Lynn & Fakenham
- ≡≡≡ Eastern & Midlands
- ▫▫▫▫ Norfolk & Suffolk Jt. C'tee

Left:
Constituent Companies Map

attractive to the parent companies because seaside resorts and holiday traffic were beginning to boom and the E&M provided access to the Norfolk coast.

Construction therefore remained in abeyance until the Midland & Great Northern Railways Joint Committee was incorporated by special Act of 9 June 1893, and from 1 July 1893, took over ownership of the Eastern & Midlands undertaking. The finishing touches to the railway west of King's Lynn were made in 1893, when a short line avoiding Spalding station was brought into service. At the same time a continuation was opened (for goods in 1893 and passengers in 1894) from Bourne to join the Midland Railway line at Little Bytham Junction, whereby a shorter route was made between the Midland system and the Norfolk coast. Until 1 January 1895, the western section (the former PW&S and the Midland & Eastern Railway) was under a manager at Spalding, and the eastern section was managed from headquarters at King's Lynn. On that date the two sections were combined under a traffic manager with offices at Austin Street, King's Lynn.

lines were left in for some time in case of a GER takeover being necessary. This section was then shortened and incorporated into sand sidings, the rest being abandoned.

From 1 January 1889 the GNR and MR became joint owners of the western section, but the E&M company in the east lurched from difficulty to crisis, under the questionable management of a Mr Read. Finally in the autumn of 1891 the GNR and MR indicated that they were interested in acquiring the rest of the E&M. The lines east of Lynn had become increasingly

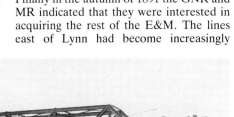

Left:
Thurne bridge, Potter Heigham, had hardly been built when this train of clerestory-roofed Yarmouth & North Norfolk Railway coaches was photographed. The little Hudswell Clarke & Rodgers 4-4-0T is either *Martham* which became successively Nos 31 and 40, or *North Walsham* which became No 32 and then No 41. Both had arrived by 1879.
Courtesy of Norfolk Library and Information Service

Below:
The M&GN System

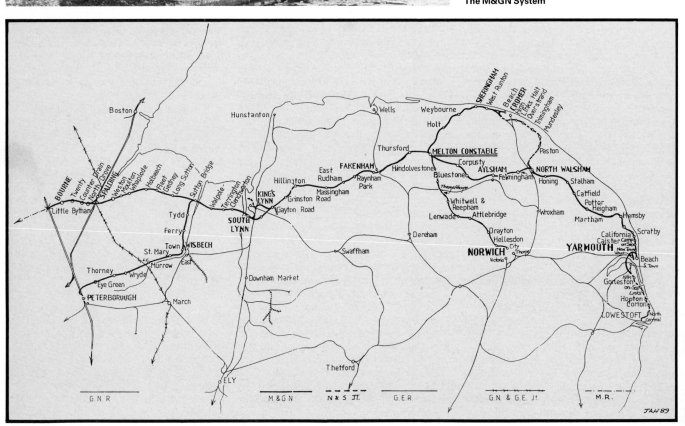

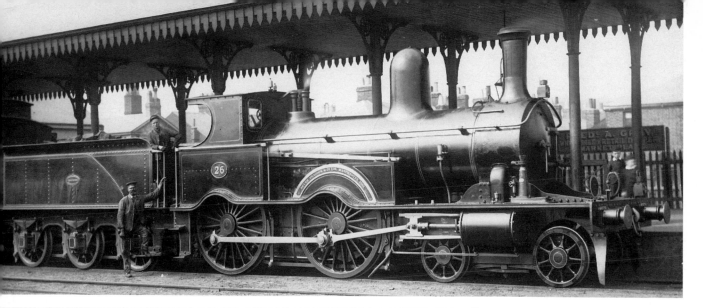

Above:
Beyer Peacock 'A' class 4-4-0 No 26 was ordered by the Lynn & Fakenham Railway but delivered to the Eastern & Midlands Railway in that company's livery in 1883. Seen here at Yarmouth Beach station early in its career with the tall dome and the built-up chimney which, it is believed, was fitted to this batch when new. In 1904 it was fitted with a MR Class C boiler and in 1923 acquired a similar boiler set higher, whereupon the cab spectacles were changed to a round design and a larger tender fitted. No 26 was the first to go to Stratford and was immediately scrapped. Note the Great Yarmouth & Stalham Light Railway clerestory-roofed brake van. *Real Photos*

Left:
As originally built for the Yarmouth & North Norfolk Railway in 1878, *North Walsham* has its slide bars covered, to keep out sand from the motion, it is believed. Sections of the line ran very close to the beach and from 1908 onwards had to be protected from erosion by the sea. These pretty little engines are a favourite prototype for railway modellers. However, every one of the class had subtle differences! *Real Photos*

Below left:
The somersault signal at Cromer Beach is 'off' as the second of the 'A' tank locomotives, No 20 built in 1909 departs with a short train.
T. G. Hepburn/Rail Archive Stephenson

In order to round off the Norfolk coast lines, a new joint undertaking — the Norfolk & Suffolk Joint Railways Committee — was established by the Midland & Great Northern Joint Committee jointly with the Great Eastern Railway; this was incorporated by an Act of 1898. A branch from North Walsham to Mundesley was opened on 1 July 1898; a line between Yarmouth and Lowestoft on 13 July 1903; and an extension from Mundesley to Cromer on 3 August 1906.

Thus from 1893 to 1923 the Midland & Great Northern Joint Railway was run by a Committee independently of its parent companies, but at the same time very much dependent upon the through traffic those companies could provide. Local traffic alone could not keep the line going: it was mainly seasonal traffic which was the lifeline (yet also the Achilles heel) of the 'Joint'. The line provided access for the Midland and Great Northern Companies to the East Anglian docks, ports and

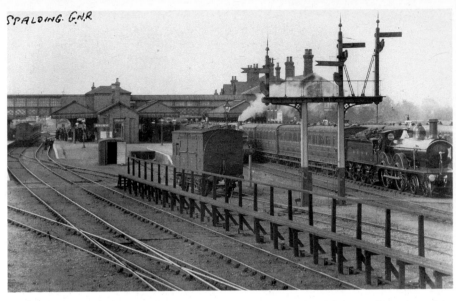

SPALDING. G.N.R

holiday resorts, and enabled agricultural produce from East Anglia to reach wider markets served by the parent companies.

By the 1920s road competition was already beginning to be felt by most railways. The 1923 Grouping appeared to bypass the M&GN for it remained apart from the Big Four, the MR and the GNR joining with the LMS and LNER respectively: the danger was that the LNER would not compete against itself by sending traffic by the M&GN. For example, the GNR train from Leeds Central to Yarmouth Beach via Barkston and Spalding never ran after 1923.

Consequently the M&GN depended more and more on the LMS while remaining an independent line with its own administrative offices. Finally, however, the administration of the M&GN was taken over by the LNER on 1 October 1936, although it still remained independently *owned* by the parent companies, and the LMS still therefore had a 50% stake in the Joint Company. The immediate effect was the closing of the traffic manager's offices at Austin Street and the closure announcement by the LNER confirmed the situation:

'With the closing of the Austin Street offices the M&GN line will still be a separate entity, but it will be worked entirely by the LNER from its Chief Officers in London through the District Officers at Norwich, Cambridge and Peterborough.'

Many remain convinced that 1 October 1936 was the day the soul finally departed from the M&GN. The situation from that date was succinctly described by no less a person than the late Gerard Fiennes OBE, FCIT who was appointed Chief Controller at Cambridge in 1935 and later, of course, became General Manager of the Eastern Region. In a letter to the *M&GN Circle Bulletin* he wrote:

'In 1936, under a deal with the LMS which did a little to rationalise Joint lines up and down the country, the LNER took over management of the M&GN and the Western end fell to the Cambridge District. It was soon obvious to me that the M&GN was staffed by East Anglians — that is to say, cheerful, humorous, loyal, dedicated, self-reliant, competent, stubborn railwaymen.

'It was also obvious that the M&GN depended almost entirely on the LMS. Certainly between Spalding and Sutton Bridge it had several 80 wagon-a-day stations. Elsewhere in all the considerable towns the old GER were in also;

Peterborough, Spalding, Lynn, Cromer, Norwich, Yarmouth. And there weren't many of these towns for 150 miles of railway. The M&GN survived on the traffic which the LMS routed to it, freight and passenger. For the LMS to do so was a relic of the competitive days. On the whole the M&GN was the less efficient route. It suffered by comparison with the GER from worse and more frequent gradients. Moreover it was restricted over two-thirds of the line to engines of route availability "4" whereas to all the principal competitive towns the GER could work the most powerful freight and any passenger engine except Pacifics. Add also that competitive distances with London were heavily on the side of the GER; and with the Midlands only slightly on the side of the M&GN it emerged that, if there were any question of the closure of either the M&GN or of the GER's competitive route it would be the M&GN which would close.

'Thus after the war and the Transport Act of 1953 the winds of road competition began to blow fiercely around our ears, and I believe it was in 1956 that John Bonham-Carter, then District Superintendent at Norwich and I came to the conclusion that one of the two routes was sufficient.

'If the decision to close was right then, it would be even more right today. More's the pity. In principle Railway Managers like running railways and dislike closing them.'

Such is a brief account of the rise and fall of the M&GN Joint Railway. Certainly, given Nationalisation of the railways after World War 2 and successive Governments' attitudes to the rail versus road debate, closure on 28 February 1959 was inevitable if perhaps a year or two premature. The M&GN was born in competition and died as the result of competition. The historical circumstances described above lead naturally to claims that the line was deliberately starved of traffic to justify closure, and certainly BR was taught many lessons from the M&GN experience on how properly to handle a closure — not all of which have been successfully remembered even to this day! Some sections of the line remained open a few years longer but the through route the M&GN created had been destroyed for ever. In our succeeding chapters and illustrations we aim to capture happier times.

3. 'Through trains to Birmingham and Leicester, the North or London'

The M&GN was indeed a through route. For a period of over 70 years you could purchase a ticket at Liverpool, Manchester, Birmingham, Leicester or Nottingham and several other big centres and ride across England in a through carriage roof-boarded 'Cromer, Norwich, Yarmouth (Beach)' or 'Lowestoft'. The daily 'Leicesters' as they were known, created the trend of Midlanders holidaying in East Anglia which is still evident to this day. From King's Cross you could also travel in a GNR coach marked 'Cromer'.

The King's Cross-Cromer service was the first through route to be inaugurated, during the Eastern & Midlands era in 1887, with three trains in each direction. By 1889 this had increased to five each way. Best times were 4¼hr (down) and 4½hr (up). Initially some trains ran via South Lynn and Spalding, the others via South Lynn and Wisbech. By 1895 the famous 3pm from King's Cross to Cromer was running, stopping after Peterborough only at Wisbech and Sutton Bridge, before South Lynn. By 1897 this train ran all the year round. In 1898 an additional through train known as 'London Sheringham — Cromer Tourist Express' left King's Cross at 1.10pm. After stopping at Finsbury Park and Peterborough the train ran nonstop to Melton Constable (where there was an incredible 3min only turn about, bearing in mind the train reversed here), arriving at Sheringham at 4.46pm and Cromer Beach at 4.55pm. The total time taken for the journey was 3hr 45min with an average overall speed of 43.6mph.

In 1908 the GNR provided new high roof clerestory rolling stock for the Cromer service. It was not taken into M&GN stock or even loaned to the M&GN, as has been stated in previous publications. Normal winter load was three coaches for Cromer, one for Norwich (detached at South Lynn), a portion for the Spalding line (detached at Peterborough) plus a Cambridge portion of five or six coaches which was detached at Hitchin.

Thus the service continued, with small variations, through the years up to 1936. All this was in direct competition with the GER, which ran express trains between Liverpool Street and its Cromer station, the most famous being the 'Norfolk Coast Express'. GER trains could do the journey from London to Cromer in 2hr 55min as the Great Eastern route was 20 miles shorter, and was without the lengths of single track of the M&GN. Liverpool Street and Cromer (GER) stations were however much less conveniently situated compared with King's Cross and Cromer Beach. The height of the competition was before 1914, when M&GN staff were under threat of fines if the Cromer Express was needlessly delayed! After World War 1 both services were retained, but in reduced

Left:
Eastern & Midlands Railway Timetable 1889.

Left:
A view near Weybourne early this century of 'A' 4-4-0 No 24 with tablet catcher extended, hauling a through GNR express. This section of the line has now been recreated by the preserved North Norfolk Railway. *Real Photos*

Centre left:
A scene near Leicester MR in the 1920s, photographed by Henry L. Salmon, showing 4-4-0 57 with large 'G7' Belpaire boiler, plain splashers, yellow livery and original two-rail tender heading a M&GN express with some variegated stock.
A. G. Ellis collecton

form. After the 1936 'takeover' by the LNER a Melton Constable-Liverpool Street service was inaugurated with through coaches from Cromer. The development of the through services from the Midlands and the North demonstrated the Midland Railway's desire in particular to provide holiday outlets for the densely populated area it served. This is revealed by the following extract from the MR's publication *Holiday Tours in the British Isles, Season 1894*:

> 'The line leading to the Eastern Counties may be comfortably approached from either Nottingham or Leicester. Travellers from the Northern and Midland Counties via Nottingham proceed to Melton Mowbray, notable, as everyone knows for its pork pies, and as a famous hunting centre. The line from Nottingham joins at this point the railway from Leicester to Peterboro', Lynn and the East. The old route to and from Norwich and Yarmouth, etc was via Stamford, Peterboro' and Wisbech, but with the opening of the new Saxby and Bourne line more direct and rapid access has been afforded to the Broads and Watering Places of Norfolk.
>
> The recent acquisition by the Midland and Great Northern companies of the Eastern and Midlands Railway, from King's Cross to Cromer, Norwich and Yarmouth, and the opening of the Midland's new line between Saxby and Bourne, has made the 'Land of the Broads' and Cromer, Sheringham, and other watering places on the north coast of Norfolk much easier of access to the populations of the Midland Counties and the North of England. The coast of Norfolk improves on acquaintance, and Cromer Beach is rapidly developing into a favourite holiday and health resort. The line passes through almost the entire extent of the broads, and is the most convenient route for the more notable parts.
>
> 'Of the merits of Yarmouth as a popular holiday resort it is not necessary to speak, as the multitudes who go there year by year are a sufficient criterion of its importance. With Cromer, however, the case is somewhat different. It is not, in the correct sense of the term, a popular resort, as the general public have not begun to flock

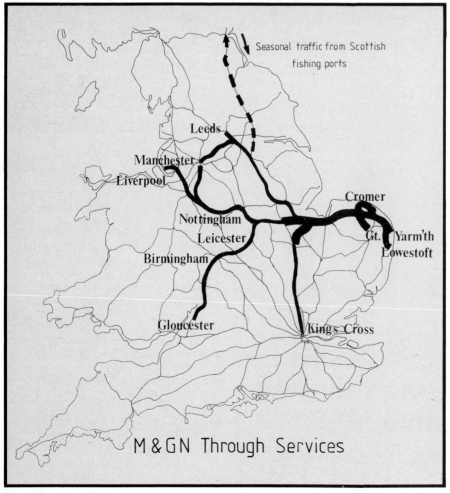

Left:
M&GN Through Services Map.

Above:
Though the LNER had taken over the previous year, the 'Leicester' was still entrusted to a 'G7'-boilered M&GN 4-4-0. No 055 has regained its splasher openings and is now fitted with a double-extended smokebox, stovepipe chimney and three-rail tender. The scene is at Hillington.
Dr I. C. Allen

Above right:
A double-headed train from Lynn to Yarmouth Beach on 23 March 1936 is seen at Melton Constable. The pilot engine is No 77, also shown in a colour plate, but now with a 'G6' Belpaire boiler and a new cab. The train engine is No 53 of the same class but rebuilt with a larger 'G7' type boiler. Note the tablet catcher. *A. W. Croughton*

there in large numbers. It is more adapted as a retreat for families, and that class of the public who are averse to a crowded watering place, and yet do not find their ideal of happiness in the solitude of the country glades and hedgerows. In other words, it hits a happy medium between the two. Inland, some of the prettiest walks may be taken and the scenery enjoyed before there is time to feel fatigued, and the beach at Cromer is an ideal spot on which to while away the long summer day.'

Thus 'Poppyland' was exploited.

The publicity was soon successful as the following personal recollection by an ex-M&GN employee demonstrates: 'One Saturday I was on duty preceding August Bank Holiday Monday and at 9pm that evening I asked Percy Webb, the signalman in South Lynn Junction Box, how many trains had passed through the station

Above right:
Rebuilt M&GN Class C 4-4-0 No 56 with G7 Belpaire boiler approaches Nottingham London Road Junction with the Cromer/Yarmouth to Manchester/Liverpool train on 13 August 1932.
T. G. Hepburn/Rail Archive Stephenson

Right:
Gresley Pacifics frequently handed over their through expresses at Peterborough North to a solitary M&GN 4-4-0. On this occasion, with express headlamps, 'Da' 0-6-0 No 083 is piloting No 044, a 4-4-0 with small Belpaire boiler, on 20 May 1938. No 083 has a new smokebox and chimney. Though bearing its LNER number, the numerals on the bufferbeam are in M&GN style and it is still lettered 'M&GN' on the tender.
H. C. Casserley

that day — the reply was 113 with the first at 3.30am!'

Tales of the performance of the old Joint locomotives are legendary with often the 'C' class 4-4-0s taking up heavy excursions brought in to Leicester by more illustrious and larger cousins. The following is a good example in 1928 recounted by a retired South Lynn guard:

'On the Friday before the August Bank Holiday Saturday, we went from South Lynn to Leicester with a train of 21 6-wheel coaches, and then lodged at Leicester. On the morning of August Bank Holiday Saturday we left Leicester at 1.32am with 16 Midland bogies for Yarmouth, calling at Melton Mowbray to pick up passengers and Bourne for water. The engine was No 52, Driver S. Wells, Fireman Bill Violin. The train was double-headed from South Lynn to Melton Constable with No 69, Driver Fitheridge, Fireman Bill Reeve. No 69 came off at Melton and the train arrived at Yarmouth nine minutes late.'

Double-heading was, in fact, an infrequent occurrence.

The years 1902 to 1904 formed the peak period of the 'Leicester' — when it took 4hr 55min from Birmingham to Yarmouth with seven intermediate stops, and 4hr 50min in the reverse direction with five regular and one conditional stop. The coaches probed even further west, as they formed a stopping train to Gloucester, from where the train returned to East Anglia the following day.

July 1908 also saw the introduction of the 'Lanky'. This train left Manchester (Victoria) at 10.5am and after a rather leisurely journey on the Lancashire & Yorkshire Railway (L&Y) reached Wakefield where it was joined by a GNR portion from Leeds. After leaving Doncaster, the train stopped at Newark, and then ran via the Barkston curve to Sleaford, thence to Spalding where the M&GN took

over. The Cromer and Yarmouth portions were divided at Melton Constable. The return train left Yarmouth at 1.32pm, Cromer at 2.5pm and Melton Constable at 2.50pm. Restaurant cars were added in 1909.

While, as explained earlier, the M&GN lost some of its through traffic after the Grouping, a new express service from Liverpool Lime Street to Lowestoft was inaugurated composed of coaches still in the L&NWR livery, so earning the nickname of the 'Ghost train'.

The various portions of the train joined or split at Melton Constable often with very little booked time in which to do it. Here is a personal recollection of the procedure:

'I remember witnessing, just after the war, the complicated operation of assembling the up express to Birmingham at Melton Constable. First the Norwich portion drew into the up platform, then out towards Fakenham; simultaneously the Cromer coaches drew into the down platform. Next the Norwich portion was backed over the West Box crossover on to the up line and on to the Cromer coaches. These two portions were then coupled up and the Yarmouth coaches were by now standing in the up platform. The Cromer and Norwich coaches were then drawn out of the down platform, over the crossover, and backed on to the Yarmouth coaches, coupled up, and so away to Birmingham.'

The use of GNR and MR bogie passenger stock, with restaurant cars and buffet cars, on the King's Cross-Cromer and the

Above:
The few ex-GE 'B12/3' 4-6-0s which were transferred to the M&GN were regularly on the through Leicester Expresses. No 61545 is seen on 6 April 1953 leaving Melton Constable on the 9.00am from Yarmouth Beach. *E. Tuddenham*

'Leicester' services respectively, gave a somewhat irregular appearance to the trains, coupled as they were to the M&GN's coaches; for after the earliest four-wheel rolling stock the coaches used for many years by the Joint were of the

Below:
'4MT' 2-6-0 No 43066 enters Saxby with 4pm Spalding to Nottingham while '4F' 0-6-0 No 44414 prepares to leave with an eastbound excursion on 26 July 1958. *H. N. James*

six-wheel pattern. A distinctive elliptical roof design was obtained by the Eastern & Midlands and some lasted to the end of the Joint. More common, however, were the six-wheel GNR pattern coaches, and these were almost the hallmark of the M&GN, smart in their varnished teak.

However by the 1930s they were proving most unsatisfactory, so much so that R. B. Walker, who succeeded William Marriott as Traffic Manager to the M&GN, was compelled to write the following letter to the LMS at Euston:

'Dear Sir,
'I feel I ought to bring to your notice the general complaints from the travelling

Above:
4MT 43088 leaves the tightly curved 'S'-shaped platform at Sutton Bridge on 27 July 1958 with an excursion from Pinxton to Hunstanton.
Dr I. C. Allen

public regarding the type and condition of our Joint coaching stock.

'You will be aware our stock is of the 6-wheel type, mostly non-lavatory, and, being old, not comfortable. Its unfavourable comparison with modern railway stock and omnibuses in the district is a serious handicap in our efforts to maintain, let alone regain, our passenger traffic.

'Verbal complaints and caustic comments from all parts of the line are too numerous to record, being almost daily occurrences, but I give below some extracts from letters and verbal protests received:'

The extracts included the following:
'If a similar type of vehicle was used in France, it would be labelled "Horses"' (Lord Hastings), 'Prehistoric passenger rolling stock used on some of your trains' (Col Clayton), 'The rattling of the coach to Peterborough made me quite ill' (Col Kennedy), 'The oscillation was so pronounced I was unable to read' (Lady Portal), 'These are the worst rattlers I have ever been in' (Sneath & Son, Grain Merchants).

A survey of stock naturally ensued and as a result secondhand bogie carriages were obtained from both the LMS and LNER companies. These included clerestory-roofed Midland and NER, flush-sided NER, and old flat-roof LNWR coaches, followed by some distinctive

GER vehicles. As can be seen from some of the illustrations, these coaches, usually in variegated formations, and accompanied by a little six-wheel brake continued to give delightful spice to the passenger services, and trains soon rivalled those on the GER section for their non-standard rakes of vehicles.

As regards motive power the Joint in the 1890s borrowed several MR 2-4-0s for working the through trains. Subsequently the Midland engines were changed at Bourne, but during the majority of the M&GN era the trains were worked right through to Leicester and Nottingham first from Yarmouth, later with an engine change at South Lynn. The Johnson 4-4-0s mainly handled the work up to the 1930s, when other locomotive types were used as noted later.

Below:
A rustic picture of Edwardian England. A Class 'C' 4-4-0 stands at Hellesdon station with a selection of six-wheel coaches of Eastern & Midlands, Great Northern and Midland parentage. Bridge spandrels were required due to miscalculations of span during construction! *Courtesy E. W. Beckett*

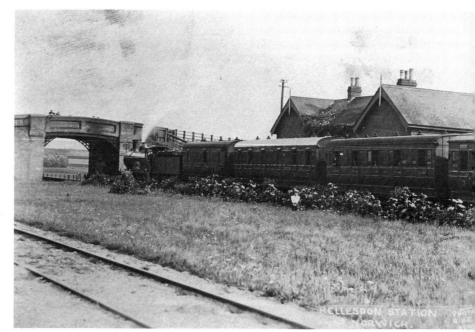

4. 'Cabbages and daffodils, strawberries and currants'

4. The freight traffic generated by the M&GN was another vital ingredient flavouring the Joint. Some commentators believe that the building of the M&GN was the result of a master plan to reach the east coast, hatched by the MR and GNR virtually from the beginning. However, as we have seen detailed study of the early history of the constituent lines does not support this, as the through holiday traffic was not generated until the 1890s.

Yet first the GNR and then the MR were involved with the early lines in the west because of their desire for access to the ports and harbours, particularly King's Lynn, but also Wisbech and Sutton Bridge en route. Indeed the GNR was directly involved in the ill-fated Sutton Bridge Dock scheme commenced in 1875. The Sutton Bridge Dock Company obtained an agreement from the GNR to subscribe for £10,000 of the share capital for the use of the dock and to pay for the terminal accommodation for the traffic. The dock was constructed and on 14 May 1881 the *Garland* entered, watched by a huge crowd. The official opening was planned for 29 June but on 10 June the lock entrance began to sink and finally caved in on 12 June. Only a handful of ships had used the dock and all attempts to rectify the matter proved abortive. The dock branch remained, but had no docks to serve. The MR also gained access to the dockside, but in the subsequent years cargo traffic was limited to off-loading from the riverbank only.

Through the Peterboro', Wisbech and Sutton branch the MR had access to Wisbech Harbour, and Wisbech M&GN Goods was unique on the Joint in having a team of heavy horses to haul wagons between the goods yards and the harbour on the River Nene about ½-mile away.

The port of King's Lynn was, however, the main goal and, as we have seen, access to it was obtained from 1867 via the GER and Lynn & Sutton Bridge Railway, and the King's Lynn Dock & Railway Company. In the early 1900s many trains were run to King's Lynn Docks with coal and pig iron, often being hauled to South Lynn by engines of the appropriate parent company.

Apart from coal, traffic from the parent companies to the areas served by the Joint

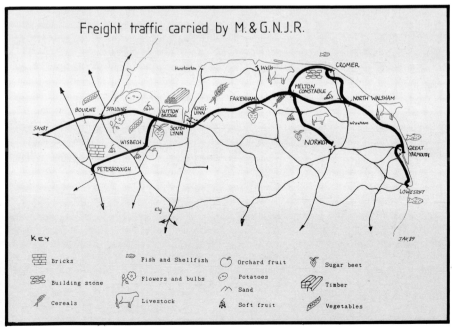

Above left:
A pleasant scene early this century at North Walsham. Class A 4-4-0 No 23 stands under the characteristic M&GN footbridge with a pick-up goods train. Note the headlamp configuration of this period. *Real Photos*

Left:
Map of Freight on M&GN.

Right:
A rare photograph of a heavy fishworkers' special at Yarmouth Beach using GNR and East Coast Joint Stock c1910. These trains brought workers from fishing ports along the Moray Firth and Aberdeenshire and GNSR and NBR coaches to the M&GN. R. B. Walker, later to succeed William Marriott as Traffic Manager, can be seen on the left. *Official photograph/Courtesy Mike King*

Centre right:
'4MT' 2-6-0 No 43110 passes East Rudham with a cattle special from Fakenham on 21 May 1958. The transport of cattle to Lynn Docks is reputed to be one of the principal reasons for the building of the Lynn & Fakenham Railway. *E. Tuddenham*

Bottom right:
'Da' 0-6-0 No 86 on a freight near Thursford, 4 July 1936 with Driver Pip Green and Fireman Alan Wells on the footplate. Locomotive has a bolt-and-clip smokebox door, stovepipe chimney and jumper blastpipe, which were soon removed by the LNER. Note also Henry Casserley's car in background! *H. C. Casserley*

was not particularly heavy. The autumn fishing season at Yarmouth and Lowestoft called for large numbers of fish vans from the MR and GNR and special trains of trawler coal, salt specials, and trains of fish barrels. (Not to mention the trainloads of Scots fishergirls!) Throughout autumn also Irish cattle were transported to the rich pastures of Norfolk.

The main feature was however the outward flow of seasonal traffic to London, the North and the Midlands. At the beginning of each year there was the flower bulb traffic. Before World War 1 the bulbs were imported from Holland to Lynn Docks but as home production grew, special trains were run from Long Sutton to serve the Spalding line and also from Terrington to Peterborough. The record for flower loading is probably held by Holbeach — 45 vans a day filled with daffodils, narcissi, hyacinths and tulips. This continued until May when the fruit season began, with first the soft fruit — gooseberries, strawberries, raspberries, red and blackcurrants. Along with the soft fruit came the new potatoes, but these were consigned by goods train whereas the fruit was 'passenger rated'. The vegetable season was by then also in full swing — lettuces, cabbages, broccoli, and large quantities particularly of green peas. Later came the plums, apples and pears, particularly from the Wisbech area. After the Western Section fruit season there was a minor season consisting of blackcurrants on the Yarmouth line.

Road competition began to take its toll between the wars but the M&GN succeeded to some extent to combat this by inaugurating a Country Collection scheme, hiring vehicles to carry the produce from farmer to goods yard, always, of course, in competition with the GER lines.

Hardly had the fruit and vegetable season finished when preparation had to be made for the fishing season at Yarmouth and Lowestoft, as already described. When the herring shoals moved south, so did the fishworkers — perhaps 16 to 18 trains of the Scots fishergirls who were to gut and pack the fish on the dockside that were boxed or loaded loose on to the M&GN for distribution throughout the country. The trail of the fish trains caused the rails to be extremely slippery for any following locomotives. Once the season had ended, the fishworkers were transported back to North-East Scotland — often in North British and Great North of Scotland Railway coaches.

From the late 1920s the remainder of the year was increasingly taken up by the sugar beet traffic. Although the King's Lynn sugar beet factory at South Lynn was the only one situated on the Joint line, factories at Cantley, Wissington, Peterborough and Spalding drew considerable portions of their supplies from the M&GN area. Sugar beet was also sent from the

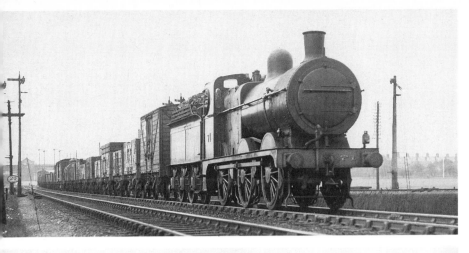

M&GN stations to factories as far distant as York, Selby, Colwick, Kelham and Felstead, as well as to Ely, Bury and Bardney. The season usually extended from the end of September to the beginning of February, thus completing a year of seasonal traffic on the M&GN, supplying produce of the Fens, Norfolk and the sea to the country in general.

There was other freight traffic of course — a huge variety as on any railway. Timber from the docks, bricks from Eye Green and Dogsthorpe, grain, coal, and later military traffic to the various airfields in Norfolk are but a few examples, but it was the conveyance of agricultural produce which formed part of the Joint's character. As befitted such an agricultural line, the Joint Traffic officials, from country station-master upwards, kept a hopeful and expert

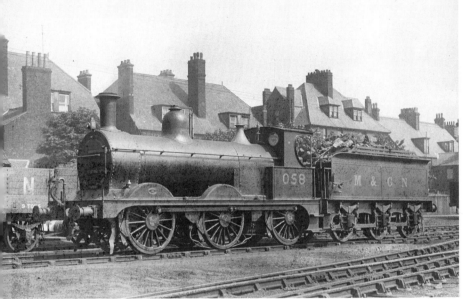

Above left:
Another mixed freight, this time leaving South Lynn for Melton Constable c1935. On the right is the local line to Kings Lynn. No 71 was one of the four 'D' 0-6-0s rebuilt with 'G7' Belpaire boilers and an extra rail on the tender. These strong locomotives hauled the heaviest loads, both passenger and goods. No 71 was one which acquired a stovepipe chimney.
L&GRP, courtesy David & Charles

Left:
The first Class D 0-6-0 stands on shed at Yarmouth on 21 June 1937. Still in M&GN livery although with its LNER number painted in yellow, it has aquired an extended cab with grab rails.
T. G. Hepburn/Rail Archive Stephenson

Below:
Class C No 43 passes Exton Road sidings with an eastbound goods train in the 1930s. Driver Jimmy Wood, on the footplate, was Secretary of the South Lynn Mutual Improvement Class.
F. R. Hebron/Rail Archive Stephenson

eye on the progress of the crops. After touring the parish and yarning with farmers, they could make a provisional estimate of the requirements of wagons, vans, sheet-vans and boxes for their station, and to many of them the weekly procession of long excursion and relief trains was a worrying diversion from the *real* work, the capture of traffic for the Midland & Great Northern Joint Railway itself.

The M&GN owned its own goods vehicles until 1928 when most were transferred to the LMS and LNER and with the common user system any wagons from the 'Big Four' could be observed. There were however a number of indigenous brake vans which remained as well as the departmental stock including permanent way vehicles. The Joint also owned some specialised wagons such as horseboxes, cranes and gas cylinder wagons.

Above right:
The first named engine for many years on the M&GN was GCR 'D9' 4-4-0 No 6021 *Queen Mary*, seen here at Sutton Bridge in 1937 hauling the 'Leicester'. It had a large dome and tablet catcher. *E. E. Boltz*

Right:
A parcels train of mixed stock near Peterborough soon after LNER had renumbered 082, a 'Da' 0-6-0 which had been fitted with a 'J4' boiler with Ross-pop safety valves at Doncaster. *Real Photos*

Below:
The 'Ragtimers' were strong but rough engines. 'K2' No 61748 in the BR regime is passing Themelthorpe with a Class B freight for Norwich City on 7 September 1949. *E. Tuddenham*

Top:
In 1957 a new company Anglian Building Products, started providing a specialised freight traffic for the Joint, namely concrete products for the building trade, manufactured at their Lenwade factory, and keeping this small section of the M&GN open to 6 January 1982. In 1958 two '4MT' 2-6-0s No 43148 and No 43147 are seen leaving Lenwade with a train of precast concrete bridge sections. *E. Tuddenham*

Above:
One of the few BR Standard steam locomotives to have been photographed on the M&GN, '4MT' 2-6-0 No 76034 is passing through Melton Constable with a freight from Norwich City.
E. Tuddenham

Right:
A fine array of M&GN road transport outside Norwich City station c1897.
Courtesy Mr & Mrs Creasey and W. C. Tuck

5. 'Elegant without benefit of paint and livery'

The locomotive workings over the lines which became the M&GN fall under distinct phases: (a) 1858-1882 under the disparate small companies; (b) 1882-1893 as the Eastern & Midlands Railway; (c) 1893-1936 as the Midland & Great Northern Joint Railway; (d) 1936-1947 under the London & North Eastern Railway; and (e) 1948-1959 under British Railways to closure of the main system.

1858-1882

The Bourne-Spalding-Lynn trains which ran along the independent lines in these districts were provided by the GNR, initially Sharp 2-2-2s, Sturrock 0-4-2Ts and in the 1870s Stirling 0-4-4Ts, but mainly mixed traffic 0-4-2s.

The Peterboro'-Sutton Bridge-Lynn passenger services were served by Midland engines, at first 2-2-2s, later Kirtley inside-framed 2-4-0s 1070/1/3; goods were worked by Kirtley double-framed 0-6-0s.

At the eastern extremities of the system, the Great Yarmouth & Stalham (later renamed the Yarmouth & North Norfolk) had its own locomotives from the outset: two Fox Walker 0-6-0STs *Ormesby* and *Stalham* later Nos 15 & 16, arrived in 1877. Remarkably, No 16 survived as works shunter 16A until 1937 at Melton Constable where it was affectionately known as 'Black Bess'.

To the west, the Lynn & Fakenham Railway took over two tiny Hudswell Clarke & Rodgers 0-4-0STs *Alpha* and *Vici* which had been used by the line's contractors. *Alpha* was eventually sold to Colman of Norwich, but *Vici* survived at Melton Constable until 1932 after long disuse minus chimney.

Above right:
One of two Fox Walker 0-6-0Ts delivered in 1877 to the Great Yarmouth & Stalham Light Railway. Formerly named *Stalham*, No 16A was for many years Melton Constable works shunter, and is seen on 24 July 1936. Known as 'Black Bess' it was scrapped at Stratford in 1937. *Canon C. S. Bayes*

Right:
***Alpha*, shown here in Alan Wells' drawing prior to its sale by the M&GN to Colmans of Norwich in 1920 and removal of the number 4A on the chimney.**

From 1877 to 1881 three Black Hawthorn 0-6-0STs were built: *Holt* (later renamed *Chairman*) to the Lynn & Fakenham, *Ida* to the Great Yarmouth & Stalham Railway (GY&S) and *Aylsham* to the renamed Y&NN. As Nos 6, 7 and 17 they lasted 20 years before two went to a Leicestershire brickworks.

The most remembered and useful locomotives of the period were seven delightful Class B 4-4-0Ts from Hudswell Clarke & Rodgers which supplied three to the Lynn & Fakenham and four to the Y&NN between 1878 and 1881. Originally named, they were subsequently numbered 8, 9, 10, 19, 20, 31 and 32. In 1886, 31 and 32 were

Above:
Black Hawthorn 0-6-0ST *Holt* **was later named** *Chairman* **and became No 6 in the Eastern & Midlands list. This and No 7 were sold in 1894 and worked at the Ibstock Brick & Tile Co. No photograph of No 7 is known. The third, No 17, became M&GN works shunter and was scrapped in 1902.** *M&GN Circle*

Right:
Four of the little Hudswell Clarke & Rodgers 4-4-0Ts were lent to the MR between 1906 and 1912 to work branch trains with former Pullman cars. This picture at Harpenden in 1910 shows M&GN No 40 repainted red and bearing the number 10 to match that of the Pullman. These locomotives later saw military war service.
Real Photos

Below right:
A rare view of Cromer Beach during the period the M&GN received three MR 0-4-4Ts in exchange for four 4-4-0Ts. They retained their numbers (142-144) but were lettered M&GN. This one is hauling three MR Bain clerestory bogies on a Mundesley train between 1906 and 1912.
Courtesy L. H. J. Ward

renumbered 40 and 41. Between 1906 and 1912 Nos 8, 10, 19 and 40 were lent to the Midland Railway to work on branch lines such as Wirksworth and Harpenden-Boxmoor each coupled to an early Pullman car. For a time they bore the same number as the Pullman attached, and were painted Midland crimson. In exchange, the M&GN borrowed three MR Johnson 0-4-4Ts — Nos 142/3/4 which retained their livery and numbers but were lettered 'M&GN', and worked between Yarmouth, North Walsham, Mundesley and Cromer.

Back on the Joint, Nos 8, 9, 10 and 40 became surplus and during World War 1 they made their way to Government defence establishments in England, Wales and Scotland, three being sold to industry after the war. No 10 *Kingsley* was retained on the Longmoor Military Railway where it was used by the Royal Engineers for

rerailing exercises and actually survived, albeit as little more than a shell, until 1953 — the very last Joint locomotive.

Always with an eye to a bargain, the Lynn & Fakenham (L&F) acquired in 1880/1 eight neat outside-cylinder 0-6-0Ts which had been built in 1874 by Sharp Stewart for the later bankrupt Cornwall Minerals Railway. The L&F bought little four-wheel tenders for them, the locomotives thus running as tank-tender engines. The locomotives had originally been designed by Francis Tevithick (late of the LNWR) for working in pairs, back to back.

In 1891 the Eastern & Midlands Railway which had absorbed the L&F and the other companies, converted four of the 'CMs' to small 2-4-0s, removing the side tanks in the process. The last of the remaining 0-6-0s survived until 1902 but the 2-4-0 rebuilds had gone by 1899. The numbers of these locomotives were: 0-6-0Ts 1, 2, 11 and 12; 2-4-0s 3, 13, 14 and 18. Nos 1, 2 and 3 were originally named *Melton Constable*, *Reepham* and *Blakeney*. It is of note that the little four-wheel tenders were retained at

Above left:
Eastern & Midlands Railway No 13, still with its old Cornwall Minerals numberplate, was purchased via the Yorkshire Engine Co and given a neat tender. In 1891 the locomotive was converted to a 2-4-0 but the tender survived as a fresh water tank in the Spalding area until at least 1947.
Real Photos

Left:
Four of the Cornwall Minerals 0-6-0Ts were rebuilt as 2-4-0s but were not a success. No 3A was the last scrapped — in 1899 — and is seen here at Melton Constable. *LPC*

various fenland and Norfolk stations as fresh water tanks for 40 years or more after withdrawal of the locomotives.

It is extraordinary that 1880 was reached with such an under-powered and miscellaneous set of locomotives, none of which had driving wheels of greater diameter than 4ft 7½in!

1882-1893

This period principally covers the Eastern & Midlands Railway when the independent lines east of Lynn were merged in one company. The locomotives associated with this era were the 15 fine and handsome Beyer Peacock 4-4-0s (Class A), with 6ft wheels and outside cylinders.

Nos 21-24 were actually built for the Lynn & Fakenham and delivered in March 1882. There then followed 25-28 (November 1883), 29-31 (November 1886) and 32-35 (May-June 1888).

The 'Peacocks', as they were affectionately known, were the first large

engines on the system and equal to their task in every way. All received larger MR type C boilers by 1909 and the first eight later acquired larger tenders. A few were fitted with tender weatherboards for tender-first working. Scrapping commenced in 1931 but five were still at work when the LNER took over in 1936. Nos 24 and 25, which were with others in Melton Constable scrapyard at the time were actually moved into the works and hybridised as a new locomotive No 025 which continued in service at the west end of the system until 1941.

Above:
Class A 4-4-0 No 30 was built by Beyer Peacock in 1886. It acquired a MR Class C boiler in 1906 and was later fitted with tablet catchers on both sides and tender weatherboard for tender-first running.
Real Photos

Below:
In 1936 the boiler of the old Beyer Peacock No 25 was fitted to the frames of No 24 and the hybrid numbered 025 by the LNER. Seen here at New England shed on 20 May 1938, it lasted until its frames cracked in 1941; the last of a famous class. The tender lasted for many years, however, as water tank at Laxfield on the old Mid Suffolk Light Railway. *H. C. Casserley*

Left:
'C12' 4-4-2Ts came on to the Joint in its latter years. Some worked the South Lynn to King's Lynn shuttle, others reached the Norfolk & Suffolk Joint lines. Here is a rare view of No 67366 with the 3.26pm Yarmouth-Lowestoft local at Hopton-on-Sea in October 1956. *E. Alger/Colour-Rail*

Below left:
The Gayton Road-East Rudham section survived the 1959 closure, being kept open for goods with one train daily each way, as shown here with a 'D82XX' (Class 16) locomotive on Whit Tuesday 1960 at Gayton Road. *G. D. King*

Right:
Potter Heigham, on the line to Yarmouth Beach, was one of the victims of closure on 28 February 1959. No 64761 is seen passing Potter Heigham signalbox with the demolition train in October 1959. *J. R. Besley/Colour-Rail*

Below:
Lenwade station on 28 April 1973, barely changed at all since closure to passengers. The very last train to run there prior to tracklifting was a weedkilling special on 16 May 1983, the tracks having laid dormant for a year. *R. King*

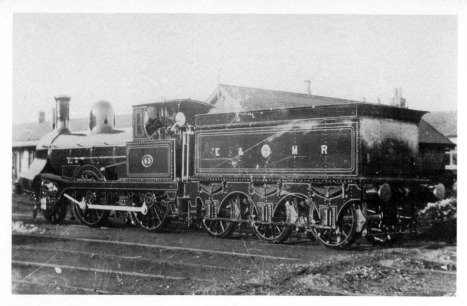

Once there were sufficient engines, the locomotive working of the lines west of Lynn was taken over by the Joint Committee and the MR locomotives, which had been stabled at Lynn since 1866 for the Peterboro' trains, were replaced. Similarly, the GNR engines left the Bourne and Lynn section.

In 1896 seven more 'C' Class 4-4-0s were delivered by Sharp Stewart (51-57) followed by 74 to 80 in 1899 but this time built by Beyer Peacock & Co.

Over the years the class received extended smokeboxes and some received larger MR boilers, at first the large round-topped 'H' boiler, and then the large 'G7' Belpaire and small 'G6' Belpaire boilers. The locomotives latterly with 'G6' boilers were Nos 2, 6, 36, 44, 49, 50 and 77. Those with 'G7' boilers were Nos 39, 46, and 51 to 57. Just prior to the LNER takeover in 1936, the resident Engineer, A. H. Nash, fitted stovepipe chimneys to several 4-4-0s and 0-6-0s, and some of the 'Cs' with small boilers were fitted with squat 'flower-pot' chimneys, and some had their spartan cab roofs extended. The 'G6' and 'G7' locomotives already had new cabs. Some engines with further smokebox extensions were also fitted with jumper top blast pipes of Great Western design. The small round-top boiler locomotives continued to the last with Salter spring-balance safety valves on the dome, whereas other locomotives had Ramsbottom valves above the firebox. A few had earlier been fitted with Ross-Pop safety valves, but they reverted to the Ramsbottom pattern.

The whole class, which for so many years had borne the brunt of the Joint's heavy traffic, lasted until the LNER took over in 1936, when scrapping began. The last unrebuilt locomotive (LNER Class D52) was No 038, scrapped in September 1943. The last G7 boiler locomotives ('D54s') were Nos 055 and 056 in November 1943; while two with G6 boilers ('D53s') — Nos 050 and 077 — lasted till January 1945.

Also in 1896 eight 0-6-0s of Johnson's standard Midland freight design were delivered by Neilson & Co — Nos 58 to 65. These were the first really suitable goods engines to be used on the line, the four-coupled passenger engines previously doing the work. A further batch, Nos 66-73 was built by Kitson of Leeds and the locomotives were delivered in 1899. Designated Class D, these engines proved to be also extremely useful on passenger duties.

Top:
Eastern & Midlands 2-4-0s Nos 42 and 43 had a long history. Built in 1857 by Rothwell for the Lancaster & Carlisle Railway, they were absorbed by the LNWR. Fitted with Webb boilers, Allan straight link motion and McConnell tenders they were bought in 1883 and lasted until about 1895.
L&GRP, courtesy David & Charles

Above:
No 78 was one of the 1899 batch of 'C' class 4-4-0s from Beyer Peacock. Although it never received a Belpaire boiler, by 1937 when the photograph was taken, it had acquired a double extended smokebox and Deeley smokebox door, an ugly capuchon chimney and extended cab, which did nothing for its looks. It is seen at South Lynn.
H. C. Casserley

In 1886, the E&M acquired two venerable 2-4-0s of the outside-cylinder Allan Crewe type from the London & North Western Railway. They had been built back in 1857 by Rothwell & Co of Bolton for the Lancaster & Carlisle Railway and had been renumbered many times. E&M No 42 was formerly LNWR *Sedgwick* and No 43 *Luck of Edenhall*. (Many previous accounts have given erroneous information on their origin.) These old warhorses did not long survive the E&M and were scrapped as Nos 42A and 43A in 1893. Yet the old McConnell tender of No 42A was

observed at Stratford as late as 22 March 1941!

1893-1936

This is the period of takeover by the Midland and Great Northern Railway Companies and the formation of the Joint Committee. Under the arrangements William Marriott who was Engineer & Locomotive Superintendent of the old E&M retained local responsibility but the GNR supervised permanent way and engineering and the Midland controlled the locomotive department from Derby. Hence the Johnson and Deeley influence.

It must be remembered that the parent companies were still operating the lines west of Lynn, and for a time after takeover of the eastern section, the lines were worked as before. However, an order was soon placed with Sharp Stewart & Co for 26 new Class C 4-4-0 express engines Nos 36-39, 42-50, 1-7, 11-14, 17 and 18 which were delivered in 1894. They were to Samuel Johnson's Midland design, inside cylinders, but with 6ft 6in coupled wheels, handsome and efficient machines which performed miracles even in almost original form until after the LNER took over.

Above right:
With a tender loaded with fire irons as well as coal and water Class C No 37 heads for South Lynn with an express c1929. The locomotive retains its Johnson smokebox door and carries the later brown livery, but with the crest still on the splasher. *F. R. Hebron/Rail Archive Stephenson*

Right:
No 060 the 0-6-0! One of the very few so numbered. It was latterly one of two 'D' class locomotives (the other one was No 073) retaining wooden buffer beams which thus could take the snowplough when required; seen here at South Lynn on 13 March 1939. *H. C. Casserley*

Above:
A five-car DMU formation enters the disused Whitwell & Reepham station on a Norwich to Lenwade railtour on 16 August 1978. This freight only link connected with the ex-GER line via the Themelthorpe Curve. *G. R. Mortimer*

Below:
Circle Members, a number being ex-M&GN employees, reminisce at Weybourne on the North Norfolk Railway as the 'J15' prepares to run around its Pullman Special train on Saturday 20 June 1987 in commemoration of the centenary of the opening of the line between Holt and Cromer Beach. *J. Hobden*

Right:
RSH 0-6-0ST *Ring Haw* passes Sheringham Golf Course in 1982 — a scene which, thanks to the efforts of the preservationists, has changed little over the past 100 years. *G. Wignall*

Apart from Deeley smokebox doors replacing the original Johnson pattern, and in the case of No 058, an extended cab latterly, all survived in original condition except Nos 62, 68, 69 and 71; Nos 62 and 69 were first fitted with large MR 'H' boilers and then, with 68 and 71 received large 'G7' Belpaire boilers. They were powerful and popular locomotives and not above tackling the through Yarmouth trains. Nos 69 and 71 gained stovepipe chimneys after which No 069 (its LNER number) was fitted with a 'flower-pot' chimney. No 071 (Class J41) was scrapped in July 1943, the last of the large boiler variety. The last small 'D' (Class J40) was No 059 which was withdrawn in June 1944: D-Day was that month too!

With the withdrawal in the 1890s of the early little tanks, Melton Constable turned out a series of nine neat outside cylinder 0-6-0Ts between 1897 and 1905. Designated Class MR, some incorporated wheels and a few other features from the old Cornwall Minerals engines. Seven of the new locomotives bore the same numbers with an 'A' suffix, but by 1907

Above:
No 62 was a Class D 0-6-0 fitted with a MR 'H' boiler in 1906, which it had until 1924 when a 'G7' Belpaire was acquired as well as a new cab with larger numerals. Note also ring handle smokebox door and safety valve cover. *Real Photos*

Above left:
One of the four large-boilered 'D' 0-6-0s, No 069 is seen at Stratford Works on 12 February 1938 after an overhaul and repaint. Note the wide capuchon chimney. *H. C. Casserley*

Left:
On 26 June 1929 0-6-0T No 93 was shunting at Melton Constable. It has 12-spoke wheels with crescent weights and yellow livery with crest. It later gained a Deeley smokebox door and a hopper. No 93 was built in 1898 and scrapped in 1944. *H. C. Casserley*

Above:
0-6-0T No 15, classified J93 by the LNER, is seen at Yarmouth on 17 May 1937 on pilot duties.
T. G. Hepburn/Rail Archive Stephenson

Right:
No 096, another of the nine neat shunting tanks, was built in 1899 and scrapped as No 8484 in 1948. It has the old 10-spoke wheels with block weights, and was the last to carry the old smokebox door. This view at South Lynn on 27 May 1937 shows the hopper fitted a few years earlier. *H. C. Casserley*

they were numbered in the series 93 to 99, the two others being Nos 15 and 16. They were useful and distinctive shunters, designated Class J93 by the LNER. Withdrawal started in 1943. Nash fitted large hoppers on their bunkers in the 1930s. After being prefixed by '0' by the LNER, five of the class were given numbers after 1947 in the series between 8482 and 8489. The last, No 8489, formerly No 16, just lasted into BR days and was withdrawn at Stratford in August 1949.

Left:
By the time No 8489 (formerly No 16) expired in Stratford scrapyard in 1949, as last of the class, the hopper had gone, the chimney was worn away, and the wheels a mixture of 10 and 12 spokes!
L. S. Lawlor

Below left:
Dubs supplied the 'Da' 0-6-0s in 1900. No 92 is seen at Melton Constable soon after delivery with its original small boiler and painted numbers which were soon succeeded by brass numerals. Note the high standard of 'spit and polish'!
Courtesy W. C. Fulcher

Whereas all other locomotives built after 1893 bore strong Derby influence, in 1900 a series of 12 0-6-0s to H. G. Ivatt's Great Northern design with 5ft 2in wheels was turned out by Dubs & Co and these engines were destined to be the last active survivors of M&GN motive power. Known as Class Da they were the only examples of both engine and tender being fitted with automatic vacuum brake. Smokeboxes were soon extended and larger boilers were fitted later to make them similar to the LNER Class J3. Nash played his new chimney game with some members of the class in the 1930s and most had a Deeley smokebox door, in some cases slightly offset. There is a photograph of one of the class with a MR chimney in 1922.

On absorption by the LNER some acquired smaller Class J4 boilers, the others being classified J3. Their larger tenders distinguished them from Great Northern examples of the class. From 1946 the LNER renumbered eight of the locomotives in the series 4156 to 4167. Old No 85 (a 'J4') actually survived until December 1951 and was the only M&GN locomotive to receive a BR number, No 64160, with BRITISH RAILWAYS on the tender.

Though found all over the system and used, like all M&GN tender locomotives, for both freight and passenger workings, the 'Das' were commoner on the west of the system. The LNER shedded some at New England, Peterborough and they were seen on normal GN section workings from that shed.

The last and unique locomotives were the 'A' tank 4-4-2Ts based on the old Beyer Peacock design. No 41 was turned out by Melton Constable in 1904 smart in yellow with oval numberplates and the railway's full title printed in an elegant crescent with full crest. No 20 followed in 1909 and No 9 in 1910, both with brass numerals. At this point, the M&GN probably had one of the most modern fleets of locomotives of any British railway:

Above left:
After 1907, 'Da' 0-6-0 No 91 had an extended smokebox to its small boiler and a wing plate from splasher to smokebox. The wing plates were to protect the sight feed lubricators at the side of the smokebox. Remarkably in 1937 its boiler plate bore the legend 'MR 1921'. *Real Photos*

Left:
Another variation on some of the Ivatt 'Da' 0-6-0s in later days was the smokebox door as on No 82, was curiously offset from the centre.
L&GRP, courtesy David & Charles

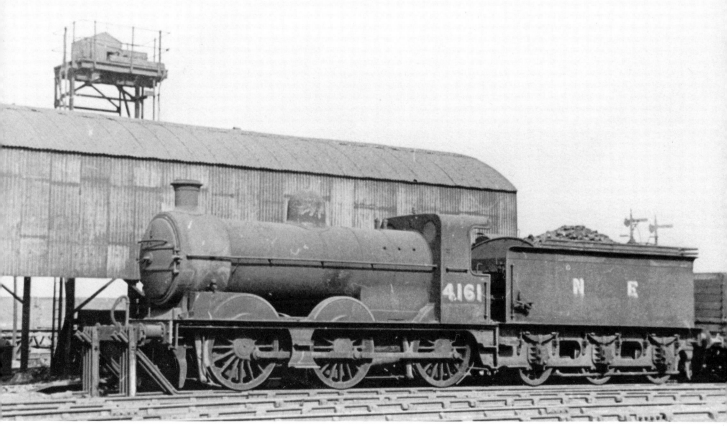

Top:
The last working M&GN locomotive and the only one to gain a BR number was Class J4 No 64160 seen here at New England on 26 August 1950. Formerly 'Da' 85 with a 'J3' boiler it lasted to the end of 1951 and had a Type C12 chimney.
H. C. Casserley

Above:
Very few M&GN locomotives survived to receive the LNER Thompson renumbering. No 086 became No 4161 and had gained a 'J6' chimney on its 'J3' boiler by 15 April 1947, when it stood by South Lynn coal stage. Within a few months it had made its final journey to Doncaster. *H. C. Casserley*

Left:
The three M&GN 4-4-2Ts became LNER Class C17. The pioneer, by then renumbered 041 had just been outshopped at Stratford on 18 September 1937. Note the cut-down side tank. *H. C. Casserley*

Right:
Another rare view at Cromer Beach in 1922, when Midland steam railcar No 2233 was on loan briefly. *W. C. Fulcher*

Below right:
The second short experiment with steam railcars was when LNER 200hp Sentinel worked holiday services in the Yarmouth area. In 1932 Conductor-Guard, the late Percy Youngman poses with Stationmaster Foster, A. L. Dorer who was second in command at the Traffic Manager's Office, Austin Street, Lynn (TMO), Mr Rivett, Driver Thompson and Fireman Walsh on the steps of No 248 *Tantivy* at Potter Heigham in 1932. *M&GN Circle*

but no further new locomotives were to appear in the further 26 years of independent existence! These handsome locomotives had 6ft wheels and were built to work passenger services on the recently opened Norfolk & Suffolk Joint lines from Cromer and Yarmouth. Two lasted until 1944 and a painting of one still graces the village sign of Melton Constable, a tribute to the last locomotives constructed in a village of little more than a thousand inhabitants — the Crewe of Norfolk.

For many years LMS locomotives, particularly Deeley and Fowler 0-6-0s and 4-4-0s worked over the Joint on excursion trains, mainly to South Lynn and sometimes to Melton Constable or beyond. Some of the Leicester '4Fs' were fitted with tablet catchers and from time to time a few were stationed at South Lynn. LMS locomotives from other depots appeared — a photograph even exists of a Bath locomotive which was itself equipped with a Whitaker tablet catcher for working the other great Joint line, the Somerset & Dorset. In 1936, two Midland '3P' 4-4-0s, Nos 758/9 were borrowed for working the Leicester Express from Yarmouth: they were well liked.

Railcars were not a feature that started with the diesel age. The MR experimented with steam railcars early in the century and one, No 2233, was photographed at Cromer Beach in 1922. In the summer of 1933 one of the LNER Sentinel Cammell steam railcars *Tantivy* worked between Yarmouth Beach and Stalham serving a number of newly opened halts close to holiday camp sites.

Other visitors in those days included at least one large Ivatt Atlantic. Great Eastern locomotives of course shared workings on the Norfolk & Suffolk Joint lines — mainly Class F3 2-4-2Ts.

During World War 1 an armoured train based at North Walsham patrolled the Norfolk coast. The locomotive was an armour-plated Ivatt 0-6-2 tank from the GNR.

By the mid-1930s the problem of an ageing M&GN locomotive stock was becoming acute. There were rumours of borrowing LNWR 'Experiment' 4-6-0s and small GNR Atlantics but nothing came of them. Tales are legion of heavy Cromer Expresses drawing into Peterborough North with Gresley Pacifics, to be taken on for their long single line ride by a puny unrebuilt Joint 'C' class 4-4-0 accompanied

by the incredulous or mocking comments of the King's Cross crew. But despite the odds, the 'C' kept time!

Then came 1936.

1936-1947

The LNER assumed control of the M&GN on 1 October 1936. The M&GN locomotives at the time were distributed as follows:

The 0-6-0ST works shunter was at Melton Constable Works, and the balance of stock was either under repair or in the scrap siding at Melton. The two LMS '3P' 4-4-0s were still on loan but were returned at once.

It would appear that on takeover by the LNER the remaining M&GN locomotive stud was regarded as having no book value. The state of the engines by this time is

4-4-0	A class	Bourne 1; Spalding 1; South Lynn 1; Yarmouth Beach 2
4-4-0	C (D52)	Cromer 1; Melton Constable 5; Norwich City 2; Peterboro 2; Spalding 3; South Lynn 6; Yarmouth 1
4-4-0	C (D53)	Melton Constable 2; Peterborough 1; South Lynn 2; Yarmouth 1
4-4-0	C (D54)	Melton Constable 2; South Lynn 6; Yarmouth 1
0-6-0	D (J40)	Melton Constable 2; Peterboro' 4; Spalding 1; South Lynn 2; Yarmouth 1
0-6-0	Dreb (J41)	South Lynn 1; Yarmouth 2
0-6-0	Da (J3)	Bourne 2; Melton Constable 2; Peterboro' 3; Spalding 2; South Lynn 1
0-6-0T	MR(J93)	Melton Constable 3; Norwich 2; South Lynn 2; Yarmouth 2
4-4-2T	A tank (C17)	Cromer 2; Melton Constable 1

graphically illustrated by the following personal recollection by Canon Charles Bayes:

'Ron Galloway used to tell a fine story of when, as a relatively junior member of the LNER motive power department, he was sent to Melton Constable to inspect the M&GN stud of locomotives. With a colleague he walked down the shed. "Actually the engines were beautifully looked after" he recalled. "They had to be!" It was like walking into York Museum. We fell into complete silence. Occasionally one of us would say something like "There's an old brown photograph of something like this at Doncaster" or "Do they really use this for traffic?" But the remark I remember was "Come and look at this one! It's got patches on the patches!"

'I still have a letter from a friend in Stratford Works headed "Requiem for 047" (The prefix "0" was placed by the LNER before the M&GN numbers). Apparently it came up for General Repairs, but they found so much wrong with it including boiler, cylinders, and crank-axle, that there was no alternative but the hammer: and that meant a replacement being found, and therefore another headache! I also heard Stratford men praise the "C" Class 4-4-0s as being very well built and maintained — but worn out.' (The remarks are a trifle unfair on No 047: it was a victim of the bombing of Norwich City station.)

On takeover by the LNER, Melton Constable Locomotive Works was closed and the responsibility for maintenance transferred to Stratford. The high casualty rate of the aged locomotives despite Stratford's efforts to repair and restore where possible meant that replacements

indeed had to be found. Unfortunately some of the replacements were as old as, and had no more power than, the engines they replaced.

The first locomotives to be transferred to the M&GN were several varieties of Great Northern Ivatt 4-4-0. 'D2s' and 'D3s' arrived on the Joint in 1936/7 to replace withdrawn Joint 4-4-0s, yet the 'D2s' were themselves built between 1898 and 1909 and the 'D3s' were even older, having been constructed between 1896 and 1899. They included: 'D2s' Nos 3042/5/6, 4321/2/7/9/35/63/68/71-6/94 and 'D3s' Nos 3400/4075/4302/6/10/5/9/45/52/5/6. Others came later. The work Joint enginemen got from these engines is legendary. A later class with a family likeness were the 'D1s'. From about 1941 some spent periods at Melton Constable and Yarmouth Beach where, as expected, M&GN men managed to perform some creditable work. Nos 3052/3/5/6/9/60/2 saw M&GN service.

The arrival in 1937 of the LNER Class D9 4-4-0s designed by Robinson for the Great Central Railway (GCR) meant that for a short time devotees could enjoy the products of those two supreme locomotive artists Robinson and Johnson on the line. Of the 22 which came to East Anglia for periods between 1934 and 1946, the following were stationed at M&GN sheds at different times: Nos 5112, 6013/4/5/8/9/21/6/30/8/40/1. As soon as they came to South Lynn the 'D9s' were put to work on the 'Leicester' and heavy excursion traffic. They appeared to be generally liked by the Joint enginemen. No 6021 *Queen Mary* was the first named locomotive to be stationed on the Joint since the early days.

The appearance on the M&GN from January 1939 of the 'D15' 'Claud Hamilton' 4-4-0s of the Joint's old 'Swedy' enemy, the Great Eastern Railway, might have appeared to be the final straw to some, but the Joint men were fair, indeed they cherished them and put them on the

full variety of tasks including the Yarmouth-Leicester workings. Later, many of the 'D16/3' Gresley rebuilds came to the Joint, some staying right through to 1959. The 'Clauds' stationed on the Joint with BR numbers where appropriate according to their periods on the line were Nos 62507/9, 8899(62510), 8884(62515), 62517, 8887(62518), 62519, 8889(62520), 8870/1, 62523, (6)2524, 62525, 8877(62528), 8878, 8862(62533), (6)2534, 62538/40, 8852(62543), 8854(62545), 8858/9, 8844, 8847(62558), 8848(62559), (6)2560, 8830(62561), 8831(62562), 8833(62564), 8834, 8837(62568), 62571, 8821(62572), 8822(62573), 8826, 8827(62578), 8814, 8801(62592), 8802, 8805(62596), 62597, 8807, 8795, 62607/8/9, 8799(62610), 8780(62612), 8782 (62613), 8785 (62616), 62617, 8789(62620).

Another Robinson design transferred to the M&GN after 1936 was the Class J11 ex-GCR 0-6-0 nicknamed 'Pom-Poms'. Nos 5222, 5323/9, 5990 and 6081 were sent to South Lynn, Melton and Yarmouth Beach sheds but did not stay long, although Nos 5222 and 5323 were about until 1942 and 1943 respectively. In 1941 No 5325 arrived and No 5990 briefly returned. They were used on passenger turns with some success. They were preferred by firemen to the 'D9s' which had high firehole doors. One 'J11' actually worked the 'Leicester' for two or three weeks without difficulty. More 'J11s' appeared in later years.

This period of course included the hard years of World War 2 with its blackout,

Below:
Ex-GER 'F6' 2-4-2T No 67228 was one of a number of the class used on the Norfolk & Suffolk Joint lines. It is seen here in April 1953 at Cromer Beach with a train for Mundesley and North Walsham; one of the last such trains before closure of the line from Roughton Road Junction to Mundesley on 6 April 1953, leaving just a short branch remaining between North Walsham and Mundesley.
Deryck Featherstone

increased traffic, shortage of supplies and manpower and general shortage of locomotives. Several other 'foreign' types visited the Joint at this time and among types shedded at various times were:

4-4-2T	C12	ex-GNR 4009A, 4015, 4502/5
2-4-2T	F2	ex-GCR 5784
2-4-2T	F3	ex-GER 8045/9/68/88/9
2-4-2T	F4	ex-GER 7076/8, 7187/8
0-6-0	J3/J4	ex-GNR 3302/45/50/87, 3850, 4033/7, 4103/13/31/43/54/5/60/2/71
0-6-0	J6	ex-GNR 3537/79/80/6/9/93/6/7/9, 3600
0-6-0	J15	ex-GER 7508/44/5/63, 7836/44, 7915/28
0-6-0	J17	ex-GER 8152/4/5/9/61/3/4/6/71/6/9/82/3/4/7/94/5/8201/2/7/8/9/11/2/5/6-8, 8220/2-4/7/9/31/2/6/8/9
0-6-0	J19	ex-GER 8141, 8241/5/7-9/51/61
0-6-0T	J65	ex-GER 7155, 7247/50
0-6-0T	J67/69	ex-GER 7082, 7194, 7339/66/90/4
0-6-0T	J68	ex-GER 7045/6

1948-1959

One of the first 'new' arrivals during the British Railways period were the ex-GNR Gresley 'K2' 2-6-0 'Ragtimers'. These locomotives were generally welcomed by Joint enginemen in spite of their 'concrete springs' as one driver described them! Most had left by 1953. The diary of Driver Nichols of Spalding for 13 July 1938 read: 'Working Yarmouth Express to Lynn with a "K2". Talk about rough!' Those shedded on the Joint were Nos 61738/42/3/8/57/66.

No 'K1s' were allocated to the Joint though they appeared from time to time.

A relatively modern type that put in an appearance was the standard LNER Gresley mixed traffic 'J39' 0-6-0. Nos 64731/61/84 and 64968 were at work between Melton and South Lynn in 1949. Others noted working east of Melton were Nos 64726/97, 64802/3/89 and 64900/13. However, the first transfer of a 'J39' to the Joint was that of No 64900 to Melton Constable on 7 November 1954.

Below:
After being worked by GNR 'C12' 4-4-2Ts, the motive power on the shuttle from South Lynn to King's Lynn was finally a 'N7' 0-6-2T. Here No 69694, auto-fitted, stands at South Lynn in August 1958. *Photomatic*

Above:
In the last years of the M&GN the GNR 'J6' 0-6-0s were familiar performers. On 15 April 1947, No 4273 stands in South Lynn with a GNR six-wheel brake and two old LNWR bogie coaches transferred to the M&GN after complaints about the six-wheelers. The signals at least show evidence of modernity. *H. C. Casserley*

From 1948, some of the magnificent inside cylinder ex-GER 'B12/3' 4-6-0s came to South Lynn and Yarmouth Beach to work principal expresses like the 'Leicester'. These large Gresley rebuilds were the first 4-6-0s to be shedded on the Joint although a GCR 'B5' was recorded on the line in World War 2, and later, standard 'B1s' and 'Sandringham' 'B2s' and 'B17s' paid odd visits. The 'B12/3s' which had spells on the Joint were Nos 61520/30/3/7/40/2/5/7/68.

No account would be complete without a reference to the locomotives which became the mainstay of the Joint in its last years and which became synonymous with the line. These were the LMS Ivatt-designed '4MT' 2-6-0s which had virtual control by 1957. They were the first really modern locomotives to be stationed on the line for some 50 years, and if ugly, were efficient and well liked. The following are among those which were photographed on the Joint: Nos 43058-63/5-8/80-3/5-8/90-5, 43105-11/42-61. The class hauled most of the final trains on 28 February 1959. Today they are remembered through No 43106 on the Severn Valley Railway.

The 2-6-0s did not quite have the M&GN to themselves. There were still a few 'B12/3' 4-6-0s and a scattering of 'Claud Hamilton' 4-4-0s: some GNR 'J6' and GER 'J17' 0-6-0s on freight workings. A few GER 2-4-2Ts were at the death of the Mundesley line: 'C12' 4-4-2Ts and then GER-type 'N7' 0-6-2Ts worked the South Lynn to King's Lynn shuttles. In the Sheringham area some large tanks like GCR 'A5' 4-6-2Ts and standard LNER 'V1' 2-6-2Ts and 'L1' 2-6-4Ts were also seen. Other types not mentioned before were 'F6' 2-4-2T, 'J66' 0-6-0T, 'J5' and 'J20' 0-6-0s. Some eight-coupled locomotives had even appeared during the war and later: GCR 'Q4' 0-8-0s and some '01' and '04' 2-8-0s and WD Austerity 2-8-0s, and at least one Standard BR Class 4MT 2-6-0. Some variety!

Dieselisation scarcely touched the Joint, but a few small 0-6-0 shunters came to the main centres, and some D55XX Bo-Bos came to the Sheringham area after the main closures. After 1957 diesel railcar sets worked between Cromer Beach and Norwich City.

And so the locomotives of the M&GN perished in their various scrapyards — the Joint locomotives to Stratford, except the 'Das' (0-6-0s) which were scrapped at Doncaster; and the odd 'J93' 0-6-0T even met its end at Darlington of all places. No M&GN locomotives were preserved, more's the shame. But a little imagination can keep bright memories of the later days by visiting the North Norfolk Railway to see its relics and the 'B12/3' 4-6-0 and 'J15' 0-6-0; York to see its 'J17' 0-6-0; Bridgnorth its '4MT' 2-6-0; and the National Railway Museum to see GER 0-6-0T. LMS Fowler Class 4F 0-6-0s are at one or two locations including No 44422 which actually worked on the Joint. An obscure Fox Walker 0-6-0ST exists to remind us of 'Black Bess', the works shunter; first cousins of the old Beyer Peacock 'A' 4-4-0s are to be found in Spain and Australia; and a few genuine M&GN numberplates are extant.

Liveries

While the 'genuine' M&GN locomotives were certainly 'elegant without benefit of paint and livery' they looked even better with!

Of the constituent lines, the Y&NN locomotives were given a dark green finish except 0-6-0STs *Ormesby* and *Stalham* which had a black livery, lined red edged cream on the inside, with red coupling and connecting rods.

On the Lynn & Fakenham Railway passenger locomotives were green with black pointings and white lines. Goods engines were chocolate-lined black-edged yellow. Generally this livery was adopted by the Eastern & Midlands Railway.

The distinctive yellow livery of the M&GN locomotive stud has been variously described as 'Autumn Leaf', 'Golden Gorse' or 'Improved Willow Green'. It clearly was one of those liveries which appeared to change according to location, light, or age. The actual production of this livery has been recorded by an ex-employee at Melton:

'After cleaning, stopping and rubbing down, first one coat lead colour priming, secondly two coats yellow ochre, then one coat of raw sienna to secure the "autumn leaf" shade, finally one coat of hard drying varnish. The 2in black bands were picked out with ¼in chrome yellow lines and, after the application of transfers, one more coat of hard drying varnish, flatted down and one coat of finishing varnish!'

The famous M&GN 'yellow', described in the 1922 Railway Clearing House *Year Book* as 'light brown', survived on all but the two classes of 0-6-0 goods engines (D and Da) until 1929. After that date the passenger engines and the rebuilt Melton Class MR tanks joined the goods engines in being painted a dark umber brown with simplified lining and large lettering. The goods engines went brown in 1925 with a short-lived sans serif style of lettering.

With the end of the yellow livery the crest was generally discontinued, though No 46 was recorded as having it for a time with its dark brown livery. The 'Da' class 0-6-0s originally had painted numerals, but soon, in common with most other locomotives, they were fitted with brass numerals. However, some locomotives carried neat oval brass numberplates. Beyer Peacocks Nos 21 to 35 had them but Nos 21 to 28 lost them on reboilering. The others with oval plates were the 0-6-0Ts No 93-99 and 15 and 16, and 4-4-2T No 41. 'Black Bess', the works shunter also had a plate with an extra brass 'A' suffix.

6. 'It gave good service to East Anglia and in return East Anglians served it well'

The operation of the M&GN system was controlled from two main centres. First, the Traffic Manager's Office, the Headquarters of the Midland & Great Northern Joint Committee was located at Austin Street, King's Lynn. William Marriott was Engineer for the majority of the M&GN's life span, and also Traffic Manager from 1919 until retirement on 31 December 1924, which led rivals to describe the line as 'Marriott's Tramway'! He was succeeded by R. B. Walker on his retirement in 1934. The Austin Street Office was in direct and daily touch with every station under the Traffic Manager's command by single needle telegraph or letter, latterly by a simple internal telephone system. On the LNER takeover in 1936 the office was closed and the 40 or so clerical staff transferred.

The second centre was the works, situated at Melton Constable: 'the Crewe of North Norfolk'. In 1881 it was an isolated hamlet of 118 people. Four years later the railway company workshops were sited there and by 1911 it had a population of over 1,150 with railway-built houses, shops, school, recreational facilities, a gas works and a sewerage station. The railway works, operating over 180 miles of track, building and repairing locomotives and rolling stock, and catering for the civil engineering needs of the system, provided employment for the majority of the working population until closure, also in 1936.

The dominant personality for so many years was William Marriott, especially in his capacity as Traffic Manager and Chief Engineer. Born in Basle in 1857 he took a position with Messrs Wilkinson & Jarvis who played such a large part in the construction of the early lines and was appointed Engineer to the E&MR in 1883. His engineering expertise manifested itself in several aspects of the M&GN, the most notable of which was his pioneering work in the manufacture of reinforced and precast concrete units. His patented Reinforced Concrete System at Melton

Works commenced before World War 1 and produced signal posts and brackets, telegraph posts, gate posts and gates, gradient, mile and fence posts, station name boards, reinforced concrete sleepers, as well as concrete bricks. These were not only manufactured for the M&GN but sold to other railways including the GNR, GCR and LNWR.

Mr Marriott was also involved with other civil engineering works on the line, notably Breydon Viaduct, over the River Yare at Yarmouth, together with the building or strengthening of other bridges including

Left:
Melton Constable around 1936. The works are to the left and 16A ('Black Bess'), the works shunter stands in front of an ex-GNR six-wheel coach. A former NER bogie coach is on the left. To the right of the ample water tank are the locomotive shed and coal hoist. Clearly a busy working day — locomotive depot looks empty!
L&GRP, courtesy David & Charles

Below left:
A demonstration length of Marriott's Precast Reinforced Concrete Units manufactured at Melton Constable Works. The photograph was taken near Melton on the down line to Holt and displays 10 different items. Many were soon commonplace throughout the M&GN system and some were adopted on other railways.
Official photograph

the North over a mainly single line railway with crossing loops, ensuring the minimum of delay, demanded a high level of track maintenance and slick tablet exchange. Consequently in 1907 the M&GN Joint Committee decided to adopt the Whitaker automatic tablet exchange system introduced on the Somerset & Dorset Joint line. The system proved extremely successful, averaging only one dropped tablet in every 5,645 exchanges.

Locomotive Running Sheds were located at Melton Constable, South Lynn, Yarmouth Beach, Cromer Beach, Norwich City, Spalding, Bourne, and briefly at Fakenham and Mundesley. The Midland shed at Peterborough was also used until 1936 when the LNER sheds were used.

Station architecture on the Joint varied according to its constituent companies, as did the design of signals and signalboxes, with mainly MR and GNR influence.

The most important ingredient forming the character of the Joint was, however, its East Anglian staff, truly it was a 'matey sort of line' and if the M&GN had a relatively short life it undoubtedly had a glorious past. It was very much a family railway with often three, or even four generations of the same family working for

Above left:
William Marriott's Inspection Saloon with No 9A, one of the neat 'B' class 4-4-0Ts which invariably worked it. Seen here about 1905 with its gleaming brass and yellow paint, it retains its Johnson smokebox door and jacks on the bufferbeam. The express headlamps are noteworthy.
Official photograph

Left:
Melton Constable Works was the Crewe of Norfolk, being the engineering hub of the M&GN. In this view about 1905, No 96, a 0-6-0T is seen in the foreground, while to the rear of the Fitting Shop are a 'B' 4-4-0T and a 'Da' 0-6-0.
Courtesy L. H. J. Ward

station itself boasted an Elizabethan building, Red Hall, utilised as a ticket office. Red Hall was traditionally associated with the Gunpowder Plot; it was probably the oldest railway building in Britain and survives today, having outlived the railway.

The requirement for fast passenger services from London, the Midlands and

Below:
An ex-GER 'F4' 2-4-2T eases down to 5mph to cross Breydon Viaduct with 10.33am Peterborough North to Lowestoft Central two days before final closure of the bridge on 21 September 1953. *E. Tuddenham*

West Lynn bridge. One of the main reasons for closure of the M&GN was the alleged weakness of West Lynn bridge, yet during demolition a diver found the original piles to be as new. Certainly however, the bridge structure was subject to weight restrictions. Other notable features on the line include Cross Keys swing bridge at Sutton Bridge, still surviving today and forming part of the A47 trunk road. The 330yd-long Toft Tunnel, west of Bourne, was the only tunnel on the system; coincidentally it equalled in length the Joint's longest platform — at Yarmouth Beach. Bourne

the Joint. It fitted men to play their part in high railway positions throughout the world.

Safety was the watchword of the Joint. Although there were some derailments and other mishaps from time to time, the M&GN claimed never to have killed a passenger in a train accident: and that is a record of which any railway could be justly proud, reflecting the care with which the system was operated and the conscientiousness of its faithful employees.

Verily it gave good service to East Anglia, and in return East Anglians served it well.

Left:
A quiet wartime scene at South Lynn shed on a May Sunday in 1940. The LNER had been in control nearly four years and ex-GNR 'D3' 4-4-0s Nos 4315 and 4319 can be seen. The M&GN however was still represented by No 052, a large-boilered Class C, and a Class D 0-6-0 still virtually in original condition, No 060. *D. H. Bayes*

Far left:
One of the oldest buildings used on a British railway, the booking office at Bourne, Lincs was in Red Hall, an Elizabethan structure reputedly connected with the Gunpowder Plot. The station footbridge can be seen on the left.
Original postcard

Left:
A Whitaker tablet catcher in action on the M&GN.
H. N. James

Below:
MR and LMS 0-6-0s were a familiar sight, particularly on summer excursions from the Midlands to East Anglia. Some Leicester '4Fs' were fitted with M&GN tablet equipment. This view c1929 shows LMS No 4418 crossing the single line West Lynn bridge (No 46) with an eastbound train. This bridge had a weight restriction which limited the power available for the M&GN main line, and the cost of essential repairs claimed by BR to be required was a major reason given for closure.
F. R. Hebron/Rail Archive Stephenson

Above:
'C' class 4-4-0 No 36, rebuilt with Belpaire firebox, leaves Sutton Bridge with a Peterborough-South Lynn train c1933.
T. G. Hepburn/Rail Archive Stephenson

Below:
Class A 4-4-0 heads east over Cross Keys Bridge with a freight train c1933.
T. G. Hepburn/Rail Archive Stephenson

Above:
The fen country suffered periodic flooding. This scene at Twenty was taken in December 1910 and shows the gradient up to the bridge over the River Glenn, which had burst its banks. A Class D 0-6-0 braves the floods with a couple of Midland six-wheel coaches and is entering the single line section to Spalding. *R. T. Ninnis collection*

Right:
Two ex-GN 'D2' 4-4-0s seen trapped with their train near Guestwick by snow during the terrible winter of 1947. *E. Tuddenham*

Below right:
The breakdown train with 'J39' 0-6-0 No 64803 about to leave Melton Constable. Note ex-NER bogie clerestory. The train had been working on the installation of a new turntable at Melton during May 1953. *E. Tuddenham*

7. 'Holiday Brummagem came — and still comes — to Yarmouth and Cromer'

Today, while the Midland & Great Northern Joint Railway was closed over 30 years ago, the spirit survives in several ways. The habit it fostered of Midlanders holidaying on the Norfolk coast still manifests itself with the Brummagem accent very much apparent amongst the Norfolk dialect during the summer months. The only remaining M&GN section along which BR trains still run is from Sheringham to Cromer, and thence via a piece of the old Norfolk & Suffolk Joint line to that of the old enemy, the Great Eastern line to Norwich.

Sheringham, however, marks the headquarters of the North Norfolk Railway which has succeeded in preserving and recreating part of the old M&GN between Sheringham and Holt. Once again the sound of steam can be heard regularly, although regrettably there are no M&GN engines. Instead two locomotives from the old rival dominate the locomotive stud. The largest is 'B12/3' 4-6-0 No 61572 designed by the GER to haul express passenger trains, the other is a 'J15' 0-6-0 No 564 a GER mixed traffic engine. The sight of GER locomotives at Sheringham is not inappropriate, for from 1906 the M&GN granted access to Sheringham to the GER when the Norfolk & Suffolk Joint line to Mundesley was jointly built, and amongst others, the GER's crack 'Norfolk Coast Express' served the resort. Today the BR line terminates just short of the original station at a simple halt less than 100yd from the preserved line.

The development of the North Norfolk Railway to its present status is a story of considerable achievement. When the M&GN was closed in 1959 the M&GN Preservation Society was formed. Initial plans to preserve sections between (a)

Below:
Happily the M&GN line from Sheringham via Weybourne to Holt is once again home to steam through the efforts of the North Norfolk Railway. Although regrettably no M&GN locomotives were preserved it is good to see the ex-GER 'J15' 0-6-0 No 564 earning its keep. It is seen here passing the Sheringham distant signal en route to Weybourne on 3 September 1978. *G. D. King*

North Walsham & Great Yarmouth, (b) North Walsham to Aylsham or (c) Melton Constable to Hindolvestone and Norwich proved too ambitious and soon floundered.

The branch between Melton Constable and Sheringham had, however, survived the 1959 axe and BR was still running trains along it until final closure at the end of 1964. The Society succeeded in purchasing Weybourne and three miles of single track from there to Sheringham. Sheringham station continued to be used by BR until 1967 when the new halt was built in its place and the Society moved into the old station. The North Norfolk Railway was floated as a public company in July 1970 and the Society changed its role from being entirely a preservation society to that of the supportive body for the company. After much hard work, particularly relaying track at Weybourne which had been abruptly lifted by BR, a Light Railway Order was granted and in July 1975 members of the public could be carried on the line for the first time. Now, at last, the line could start earning revenue in addition to relying on donations and other fund-raising activities.

Efforts continued to consolidate the running of regular services between Sheringham and Weybourne and once this was achieved work commenced in 1982 on the reopening of the section towards Holt, thus extending the railway by a further 2½ miles. It is planned to build a new station there, based on the original M&GN design and, indeed, it is not generally known that the original station at Sheringham was very similar.

As noted in an earlier chapter, the Holt-Cromer Beach section was opened by the E&MR on 16 June 1887 and, as built, the two stations were of very similar design. (Both also had very tall signalboxes as did Cromer Beach.) Sheringham's station buildings on Platform 1 were, however, extended in 1896 and these extensions included the addition of the verandah. Furthermore the original small 'waiting shed' building on Platform 2 was replaced in 1897 with improved accommodation and it was transported to, and rebuilt at, Eye! Further alterations were executed at Sheringham in 1905/7 in connection with the building of the Norfolk

& Suffolk Joint line and access to Sheringham by the GER. The original brick road overbridge was also replaced with the present well known structure and the tall signalbox demolished. What with subsequent alterations by BR in 1953 (additional facilities resulting from the closing of Cromer High station) and 1964 (economy cuts), together with subsequent changes and rebuilding by the North Norfolk Railway, Sheringham must be one of the most altered stations of its size in the land!

On leaving Sheringham station, trains on the North Norfolk Railway go under Bridge 305, built in 1906 as noted above, pass on the landward side the operating signalbox (removed from Wensum Junction at Norwich), while opposite are the original carriage sidings from M&GN days. Once the train has passed over a private road crossing, the golf course and sea come into view. Should any present-day golfer curse the distraction of your passing train, he will do well to be reminded that in 1920 Joyce Wethered, later Lady Heathcoat Amery, sunk an English Championship winning putt on the 17th green which overlooked the line, just as a M&GN train steamed by. Later she was asked how

Above:
Sheringham station buildings were extended in 1897 and this view is taken after that date. Note the tall signalbox which enabled the signalman to see over the original brick road bridge, and the original short length platforms. Further extensions commenced in 1904 in connection with the granting to the GER of running rights into Sheringham and on replacement of the original bridge by the present version in 1906, the tall box was demolished. *Courtesy B. Ridgway*

Below:
A nice view of a M&GN freight train passing through Sheringham before 1931 with Class C 4-4-0 No 1. The second road bridge is in the background. *Real Photos*

Left:
DMUs and diesels only appeared on the M&GN in its very last days. A service from Norwich Thorpe via Cromer, Sheringham and Melton Constable to Norwich City commenced on 16 September 1957. Nos 79063 and 79279 comprised the first train.
Courtesy B. F. Eke

Below left:
An 1895 scene near Sheringham with 'A' class No 29 bringing a train of six-wheelers over flat-bottomed track witnessed by two early spotters. The original Sheringham road bridge is in the background. There is no evidence of distraction on the golf course.
L&GRP, courtesy David & Charles

much military traffic. Deep water close inshore at Weybourne made it a potential invasion target. The Society has its bookstall here on Platform 1. The large goods yard now includes a locomotive shed and workshop brought from Norwich City station. The signalbox on Platform 2 had been moved from the former Holt station.

Onwards, the more recently reopened line passes under Bridge 302, then over Bridge 301. Fine views of Weybourne and the sea soon reappear. The site of Kelling Camp halt is reached, this served a large caravan park. It was a new halt built by the NNR, there being no M&GN predecessor.

Beyond the halt the line climbs a lengthy gradient of 1 in 80 on to spacious Kelling Heath with heather and gorse making splashes of colour when in flower. A new halt is proposed to give access to Kelling Park Hotel and the Weybourne to Holt road.

Towards Holt the line now passes through woodland. To the north of the line can be seen the gravel pits from which material was extracted for the construction of the original railway, and for subsequent track reballasting. A short distance before the terminus, the railway land widens, marking the area where the original Blakeney branch was planned, but never laid.

The new Holt terminus, situated a mile from the town centre and close to the bypass will again have a precedent from Eastern & Midland days for as we have seen, it was almost three years before the line was continued from Holt to Cromer Beach. The original temporary terminus is interesting, for it was the old wooden station from Yarmouth Beach with a sleeper platform. When replaced by the second station on 2 November 1886 the wooden building was moved to Melton Constable. A section survives to this day, and is the home of the local Girl Guide Association.

The second Holt station building — the one which closely resembled the original

much of a distraction it had been, to which her response, clearly having been oblivious, was the now immortal 'What train?', a query which still survives today in golfing folklore. (*Daily Telegraph*, 25 February 1987.)

Many visitors are surprised by the hilly terrain, as the train is now climbing a 1 in 97 gradient, levels off, and then briefly descends at 1 in 100. Soon an embankment carries the track to a bridge over the A149,

a bridge which was reconstructed in 1984 and serves as a memorial to NNR volunteer and experienced bridge engineer David Pinkerton who died following an accidental fall when it was almost completed.

Now there is a gradient of 1 in 80, lasting until Weybourne station is reached. This station was not, in fact, opened by the M&GN until 1 July 1901 and for many years a large army camp nearby created

Above right:
A view of the earliest days of preservation at Sheringham. The 'J15' and 'B12/3' were delivered by rail on 4 June 1967 and are seen being hauled through the platforms on arrival. *Brian Fisher*

Right:
During 1988 a railbus service operated over the NNR to Holt, pending completion of the run-round to enable locomotive-hauled trains. On 19 August railbus E79960 stood in the platform. *Paul Barber*

Above:
**The shape of things to come on the NNR: 'B12/3'
No 61572 stands at Sheringham with 'fire' in
smokebox, prior to dismantling for restoration.**
Tim Stephens

building at Sheringham — was itself
destroyed by fire in 1926, resulting in
complete rebuilding to a new design using
the patented Marriott concrete bricks and
steel window frames.

On returning to Sheringham station the
visitor can inspect an original W. H. Smith
bookstall from Waterloo station, a non-
operational signalbox originally sited
alongside Station Road level crossing,
souvenir shop, railwayana exhibition vans
and obtain refreshments from the modern
buffet on Platform 1.

Thus in many respects, history can be
seen to be repeating itself on the NNR for
holidaymakers from the Midlands and,
indeed, all parts of the country to enjoy.
The rolling stock here is too numerous to
list, but apart from the 'J15' and 'B12/3'
there are several former industrial steam
locomotives, railbuses and diesel locomotives. Coaching stock includes a L&Y
saloon, a beautifully restored Gresley
buffet car, ex-Brighton Belle Pullmans, a
LNER Quad-art set and many others.
Goods and engineering vehicles are well
represented and there is a museum and
bookstalls. As with any preserved line
futher support, both physical and financial,
is always greatly welcomed. The Registered Office of the North Norfolk Railway
is Sheringham station and the Membership

Secretary for the M&GNJR Society is Mrs
C. Ingram, 53A Ravensbourne Park
Crescent, Catford, London SE6 4YG.
Please enclose a stamped addressed envelope. The Society produces a quarterly
printed magazine for all members known
as *Joint Line.*

The M&GN CIRCLE, many of whose
members support the North Norfolk
Railway, is however a completely separate
and independent body devoted to record-
ing the memory of the original railway.
Formed in August 1959 — the year of
closure — following the placing of an
advertisement in the *Model Railway
Constructor,* it has over the past 30 years
succeeded in producing nearly 350 monthly
Bulletins resulting in the M&GN being one
of the best documented of any railway
company in the British Isles. Occasional
booklets are also produced. All this has
been made possible by the fact that the
membership which currently totals over
300 has always included many employees
of the Joint before LNER takeover in
1936, with many more also employed on
the line between 1936-59. Consequently
much information which might otherwise
have been lost has been safely recorded,
together with many rescued relics, docu-
ments and a photographic collection
currently standing at over 20,000 nega-
tives!

Drawings of locomotives, rolling stock
and buildings are also produced, as many
ordinary members are keen modellers of
the Joint. Genuine devotees of the M&GN
and former staff are always welcome to
join. The Membership Secretary is Mr G.
L. Kenworthy of 16 Beverley Road, Brun-
dall, Norwich NR13 5QS. Please send a
stamped self-addressed envelope as
before.

Bibliography

The principal general histories and
descriptions of the M&GN are in:

*A Short History of the Midland & Great
    Northern Joint Railway,* R. H. Clark;
    Goose 1967
*Scenes from the Midland & Great Northern
    Joint Railway,* R. H. Clark; Moorland
    1978
*The Midland & Great Northern Joint
    Railway,* A. J. Wrottesley; David &
    Charles 1970
*The Midland & Great Northern Joint
    Railway,* John Rhodes; Ian Allan 1982
Forgotten Railways: East Anglia,
    R. S. Joby; David & Charles 1977
The Norfolk & Suffolk Joint Railway,
    R. S. Joby; Klofron 1975

*A Regional History of the Railways of
    Great Britain. Vol 5: The Eastern
    Counties,* D. I. Gordon; David &
    Charles 1986

The best succinct account of the locos is:
The Locomotives of the M&GN,
    Alan M. Wells; Historical Model
    Railway Club & M&GN Circle 1980
An entertaining diary is:
Forty Years on a Norfolk Railway,
    M&GNR Society 1974

A number of picture albums of varying
quality have also been published.
In magazines, the M&GN histories have
included:

P. C. Dewhurst in *The Locomotive* 1921-22
E. L. Ahrons in *Railway Magazine* 1923

F. H. Gillford in *Railway Magazine* 1936
Marcus Newman in *Trains Illustrated* 1955
and, on the Norfolk & Suffolk Joint:
E. Tuddenham in *Railway World* 1966.
An excellent summary by Derek
Middleton ARIBA is in the *Railway
Observer* for April 1959, and two fine
series of articles on the locomotives by
Alan M. Wells can be found in issues of the
Stephenson Locomotive Society Journal in
1942: and in *Railway Pictorial* in 1950,
continued in *Railways* in 1951.
M&GN Circle publications include track
surveys, *Running a Railway,* personal
histories, the *Photograph Catalogue* and a
monograph by Alan M. Wells on Cornwall
Minerals Locomotives. Others are in
preparation.